End Your Marriage Peacefully

Manisha P. Patel has provided extraordinary representation in helping me navigate the very challenging phase of my divorce. She has been completely forthcoming and willing to offer her expertise and guidance throughout this difficult process. I trust her completely. She is an ethical and brilliant lawyer.

V. H.

Manisha is a spectacular attorney! She brings a unique, client-driven, collaborative perspective to the table that is impactful in today's highly litigious climate. She takes the time to intentionally listen to her clients and addresses their needs accordingly. This meaningful approach resonates throughout the firm and creates a calm, effective environment for clients. I wouldn't hesitate to reach out to Manisha for stellar representation!

M. G.

If you're looking for a legal superstar, look no further than the Law Office of Manisha P. Patel, PLLC! I had the best experience working with Manisha and her amazing team. From the moment I walked in, I knew I was in good hands.

Manisha Patel is the real deal. She's incredibly knowledgeable and has a knack for breaking down complicated legal stuff into terms that actually make sense. I felt so comfortable and confident knowing she had my back.

The whole team is top-notch. They were always on the ball, super responsive, and kept me in the loop every step of the way. I never had to wonder what was going on with my case because they made sure I was always informed.

Manisha's strategic mindset and attention to detail were game-changers for my case. You can tell she genuinely cares about her clients and goes above and beyond to get the best results. Her expertise shone through at every turn, and I couldn't have asked for a better advocate.

I highly recommend the Law Office of Manisha P. Patel, PLLC, to anyone who needs legal help. Manisha and her team are total pros who combine professionalism with a personal touch. They made a huge difference for me, and I'm so grateful for their support.

Thank you, Manisha, for being an absolute rock star and making a positive impact on my life!

O. R.

I hired Ms. Patel to represent me in a family law-related matter after receiving a recommendation from another local lawyer. I am an attorney, so I am highly selective about legal representation. Ms. Patel was professional, knowledgeable, responsive, and caring. She earned my trust during her work on my matter, and I now recommend her to friends and colleagues who need a family lawyer.

J. M.

End Your Marriage Peacefully

YOUR GUIDE TO SUCCESSFUL COLLABORATIVE DIVORCE IN NORTH CAROLINA

MANISHA P. PATEL, ESQ.

COMMON GOOD PUBLISHING

End Your Marriage Peacefully
Your Guide to Successful Collaborative Divorce in North Carolina

Published by

COMMON GOOD PUBLISHING

Common Good Publishing
Greensboro, NC, U.S.A.

LAW / Alternative Dispute Resolution
LAW / Family Law / General
LAW / Family Law / Divorce & Separation

Editing: Karen Hunsanger
Proofreading: Terry Stafford
Book Design: PearCreative.ca

Quantity Purchases: Companies, professional groups, schools, clubs, and other organizations may qualify for special terms when ordering quantities of this title. For information, email info@lawofficeofmpp.com.

Patel, Manisha P., Author
End Your Marriage Peacefully
Manisha P. Patel
Library of Congress Control Number: 2025921434

ISBN: 979-8-9935493-0-9 (paperback);
ISBN: 979-8-9935493-1-6 (hardcover);
ISBN: 979-8-9935493-2-3 (ebook).

Dedicated to the trifecta:
Adrienne Lewis, Carlie Devaney, and Christon Halkiotis.

You are my compass, my chorus, and my courage. Thank you for turning the hard days into possible ones.

Contents

Foreword 1
Invitation 3
Introduction 5

CHAPTER 1
The North Carolina Divorce Landscape 11

CHAPTER 2
The Collaborative Family Law Framework 35

CHAPTER 3
Nonviolent Communication in Practice 53

CHAPTER 4
The Mediation Process 69

CHAPTER 5
Alternative Dispute Resolution 89

CHAPTER 6
Choose Your Own Adventure 103

CHAPTER 7
What About the Children? 119

CHAPTER 8
Litigation 139

CHAPTER 9
That I May Serve 147

CHAPTER 10
Planning for the Future 165

References and Resources 173
Glossary 175
Author's Note 185
Acknowledgments 187
About the Author 191

Foreword

Every lawyer faces angry clients going through divorce. Most often, they respond with a litigious approach. This book offers a better path.

As a former family law judge and Chief Justice of the Supreme Court of North Carolina who has seen many families in divorce, I've watched family law practitioners struggle with this. I met Manisha in one of her many leadership roles among committed lawyers.

What sets this book apart is it guides the reader step by step through the collaborative family law process, demystifying what can otherwise be a lengthy, overwhelming process. The parties work toward solutions in a collaborative family law model to achieve outcomes courts often cannot.

Manisha's commitment to collaborative law is evident throughout these pages. She brings not only deep legal skills and training, but also an unwavering respect for the human experience of divorce. Her work considers how life will look after separation. Whether addressing issues of parenting, property division, or even the sensitive question of pet "custody," Manisha recognizes that families come in many forms, and that every dispute deserves thoughtful, personalized care.

This book invites clients and practitioners to understand the collaboration model, explaining legal terminology in plain language and attempting to instill confidence in the reader to achieve successful outcomes. In those cases where litigation is necessary, Manisha has the experience to strategically use trial as one of many tools available within a broader framework of resolving the disputes.

Hurt, grief, and disappointment need not dictate outcomes. With the right communication techniques and professional guidance, parties can navigate negotiations in a way that preserves relationships where possible, particularly for their children's best interests.

This book is a must-read for lawyers, clients, and anyone looking for a better understanding of collaborative family law. It reflects Manisha's deep respect for her clients' journeys and her belief that even in moments of profound change, there is room for humanity, cooperation, and hope.

Chief Justice Cheri Beasley

Justice Sandra Day O'Connor Professor

Greensboro, NC

January 2026

Invitation

Welcome! You are in the right place if you're looking for clarity—not noise—during a difficult and uncertain time. This book will walk you through what matters most when navigating divorce in North Carolina.

Information is most useful when you can *apply it*, step by step, to your own situation. That's why I've created an easy-to-follow guide, **"10 Steps to Successfully Navigating Divorce in North Carolina."**

It's designed to help you understand the legal landscape you're facing, prepare for key decisions before emotions take over, and avoid common mistakes that can cost you time, money, and peace of mind.

You can access it here:

lawofficeofmpp.com/freeguide

Let's begin with clarity, preparation, and a plan to end your marriage peacefully.

Introduction

In my very last custody litigation case, I began to fear for my life.

Initially, the opposing party was represented by an attorney who was aggressive and somewhat threatening. Eventually, they hired a second attorney, but that lawyer shifted their practice, leaving the opposing party to represent themselves. That is when things got ugly.

One day in court, the judge heard someone yelling at me in the hallway. That person had multiple documented domestic violence protective orders issued against him—not safe by any measure. The judge sent a deputy to tell him to leave, then made me wait inside the courtroom for fifteen minutes before having an escort walk me to my car.

After the custody portion of the trial concluded, I was loading my car outside the courthouse when the opposing party pulled up right in front of my car. I recognized the vehicle from trial discovery. As I loaded my car with my trial boxes and bags, they moved behind me so close that I could see the whites of their eyes in my rearview mirror.

It shook me. I drove around in circles downtown until they finally stopped following me. Then I felt safe enough to park at my office building.

I was also facing a cancer diagnosis around that time. (I am optimistic that I will soon be cancer-free.) But those two experiences—the cancer diagnosis and that close encounter with a dangerous opposing party—forced me to reassess my career. I knew that something had to change. I was done putting myself in danger.

I now focus almost entirely on non-litigation matters, primarily collaborative family law. I strongly support this non-adversarial process for divorcing couples. The specially trained lawyers work together, focusing on cooperation, open communication, and shared problem-solving.

Many attorneys here in North Carolina have completed the basic fourteen-hour training, but only a small handful of lawyers center their practice on it. I am one of them, and for most clients facing family law disputes, it will always be my first recommendation.

Since opening my practice over seven years ago, I've fine-tuned the way I select cases. I don't accept every case that walks through the door. It has to be a mutual relationship. They're hiring me, but I also want to "hire" them as a client. Because of that filter, I can take care of my clients in a way that feels personal.

What really sets us apart from other firms is that we are people-oriented. We focus on our relationships with our clients and their relationships with their family members. You will never be just a number or tick mark in our client ledger.

Sometimes it's just about walking with clients through big emotional shifts. We've had clients who reconciled with their partner, put their case on hold, and then separated again. I remember one client who apologized, saying, "I hope you're not judging me for going back to him. I'm sorry, I'm all over the place." That's not our role. We're not there to judge. We're there to help.

That idea takes me back to my 2019 commencement speech to the Economics Department at Virginia Tech. The theme I spoke on was service—specifically, serving others. Virginia Tech's motto is "Ut Prosim," which means "That I May Serve." It's always been a guiding hallmark of my life. In that speech, I said:

> "My parents instilled in me the importance of service at a very young age, urging my siblings and me to volunteer at the local YMCA, library, hospital, and science museum. This was how we spent all of our summers and school breaks. Little did I know that my choice of higher education would hold this value to a higher degree that would weave throughout my life and the choices I made. Ut Prosim means "That I May Serve." This motto not only supplemented what my parents instilled in me at such a young age, but during my four years here, I also learned how this will ultimately be the foundation and guidepost for my personal and professional life. Serving my clients, my community, my profession—this is what it is all about."

That commitment to serve has never left me. When I was younger, it was through volunteering with my family. As an undergraduate, it became deeply ingrained in me. And as a lawyer, it remains the center of everything I do. I've known for a long time that I wanted to practice law, but more importantly, I knew I wanted to use that practice to serve others.

Part of that is understanding that not every client comes to me from the same starting point. My job is to meet them where they are, whether that means setting up a payment plan, offering extra support, or simply walking them through a hard time. And when I say, "extra support," I mean it without any judgment. Some clients require more guidance and more reassurance, and that's okay.

Certainly, other attorneys have been doing collaborative law much longer than I have. However, I believe the primary difference between those attorneys and my firm, whether they focus solely on collaborative or other non-litigation matters, is that I still take on some litigation matters. As a result, I am very aware of the general court climate at any given time.

I had a call once with an opposing counsel who was also a collaborative attorney, which I like to call a "collaborative colleague." In a thirty-minute conversation about two cases we had together, he told me at least three times how I'm more in the know about what's going on with the court system and how my client receives the litigation perspective from me as well.

Keeping a small percentage of litigation cases affords me a more realistic perspective on a client's options when it comes to different forms of dispute resolution, especially collaborative family law. Because I know what it's going to be like if they have to file a lawsuit.

That perspective matters to me because it's one of the two triggers that completely changed how I practice law and led to the eye-opening moment when I realized I needed to set professional boundaries. And once I changed the way I practiced, it had this domino effect on the rest of my life: how I lead in other groups, how I work as part of a team, and even how I allow myself to be led in other organizations.

As you read this book, you will discover exactly what you need to know to create a peaceful ending for your marriage. You will learn what options are available to you in the Tar Heel State as we do a deep dive into collaborative family law, alternative dispute resolution, and mediation, and litigation options.

You will get a clear understanding of **nonviolent communication (NVC)** and how having this skill contributes to effective collaboration during a divorce. You will see that it is possible NOT to go into debt when ending a marriage, and you'll gain insights into the way custody matters are handled in North Carolina. (Hint: Your fur babies are not considered dependents.) You will have the opportunity to "choose your own divorce path" to see what options lie ahead for you. And finally, you'll find guidance on how to move forward in your new life.

Throughout these chapters, I am here to help you understand the complexities of what lies ahead for you. To make it easier, I've included a glossary at the end, which details some of the legal terms I've used. To easily identify those terms, they are in bold throughout the book.

Of course, if you have any questions about any part of the book, I invite you to reach out to me.

Manisha

CHAPTER 1

The North Carolina Divorce Landscape

Many people believe that in North Carolina, getting a divorce is as simple as wanting one, and that's it. However, the process here is similar to what you'll find in many other states. There are residency requirements, and there's a waiting period before you can officially file for divorce. In North Carolina, you have to be legally separated before you can obtain a divorce. This is referred to as a **no-fault divorce**, or an **absolute divorce**. It might sound like there are fault factors involved but there aren't.

Essentially, once you meet the statutory requirements for divorce, it's difficult for someone to contest it unless there's been a lie about one of those requirements. The two main requirements are that either spouse must have been a resident of North Carolina for at least six months preceding the filing of the divorce lawsuit, and you must be legally separated for at least a year by living separate and apart. I always tell people it's a year and a day at minimum. To be legally separated, you need to live apart; that means two separate domiciles, two different roofs. It's even been litigated that living in a camper on the same property doesn't count as living separate and apart. Similarly, having two separate bedrooms in the same house does not qualify either.

Don't mistakenly think that simply not sharing a bed means you're separated. That's not the case. The first step is to live completely separate and apart. Additionally, at least one spouse must have the mental intent to no longer live as a married couple. This means not holding yourselves out as married. Common examples of this misunderstanding include couples going on family vacations for the kids' sake or having weekly dinners together. While it's understandable that people want to maintain some normalcy, these actions can complicate matters.

In North Carolina, judges can consider these factors when determining if a couple is truly living separate and apart. If you're still engaging in activities together, such as weekly dinners or family vacations, that can reset the one-year clock. In my consultations with potential clients, I often find it interesting to explain that many actions can restart the clock. However, our appellate courts have ruled that isolated incidents of sexual relations do not reset the clock. So, if you're maintaining a continuous intimate relationship while living separately, that will certainly restart the clock, but one interaction over twelve months won't be enough to do so.

Your Judicial District

When it comes to navigating the judicial landscape in North Carolina, it's essential to understand how the system is organized, especially in the county where you reside. Each of North Carolina's 100 counties has its own courthouse, but the state is also divided into judicial districts. These districts may encompass multiple counties, or, in the case of larger counties, multiple judicial districts. For instance, Guilford County, which includes Greensboro, has two judicial districts. In contrast, Wake County, home to our state capital, Raleigh, is just one judicial district. Mecklenburg County, where Charlotte is located, is another large judicial district.

This diversity means that the **litigation** process can vary significantly from one district to another. It's crucial to discuss with potential clients what the litigation process looks like, specifically in their jurisdiction, as lawsuits must be filed where at least one spouse resides. If there are children involved, the lawsuit should be filed where the children live, which is typically with one of the parents.

If parents live across county lines and share custody equally, the choice of where to file may be based on convenience or preference. It's important to find an attorney who not only suits your needs but also practices in the appropriate jurisdiction. Any attorney licensed and in good standing with the North Carolina State Bar can work in any county or judicial district in the state, so ensuring a good fit is vital.

Each judicial district, whether it comprises a single county or multiple counties, has its own set of rules. They operate on different calendaring systems and may require various financial affidavits, disclosures, and discovery rules that can differ significantly from those in neighboring counties. I wouldn't say that one county is better than another, but certain counties might be preferred based on how they schedule cases and how long it takes for a case to be heard by a judge.

The composition of the district court bench is also crucial. For example, one county may have fourteen judges, while neighboring counties may have only four judges across two different counties. This disparity can create unpredictability about which judge will be assigned to a case, as well as the judges' experience level in civil and criminal courts before sitting on the bench. Some judges may have spent their careers in the district attorney's or public defender's offices, while others might have only worked in civil law. Some may have little to no experience in family law.

These nuances make it essential to determine the best county, or venue, for filing your case. If all parties agree to file in Guilford County, for example, we can proceed without issue. As long as there are no objections and everyone is on board, the court usually won't dismiss the case.

In North Carolina family law, all decisions will ultimately be made by a judge assigned to your case. Since the beginning of 2025, the judicial branch adopted a one-judge, one-family system aimed at providing consistency throughout the litigation process for families. While some judicial districts have dedicated family courts, many don't. Instead, family law cases are mixed in with regular civil matters.

As we embrace this new system, we have yet to encounter situations where a judge assigned to a case retires or is not reelected. This potential for change raises concerns among family law practitioners. Choosing litigation comes with its own set of challenges, and it's important to be aware of these nuances as you move forward.

How Do You Get Divorced in North Carolina?

To start the divorce process in North Carolina, it's important to first meet the requirements for **legal separation**. Many individuals come to me with questions like, "How do I start this process?" or "My spouse moved out—what does this mean for me?" They often express concerns about access to finances and their rights under the law. Let's focus on the scenario of someone who wants to get divorced but is unsure how to begin.

It's best to start with an explanation of legal separation in North Carolina. A common misconception is that you need a legal **separation agreement**, like a signed contract, before you can claim you're legally separated. I counsel clients that while having a separation agreement is beneficial, case law indicates you can enter into one even before physically separating, as long as there is intent and a plan to live apart in the reasonable future. I interpret "reasonable" to mean within about thirty days of signing the agreement, which is a good rule of thumb to share with people.

When a couple decides to separate, one person typically needs to move out of the marital home. If one spouse wants to leave but can't, we explore solutions to help make that possible. There's often a lot of emotion involved, especially if one person wants the other out of the house. In these situations, where parties can't agree on the terms of a formal legal separation agreement, I recommend creating a non-abandonment agreement. This agreement states that both parties acknowledge the need for one of them to move out and agree not to claim abandonment in court regarding issues like **post-separation support** or **alimony**. This approach can help alleviate some tension and provide peace of mind during a difficult time.

In the past year, I've seen an increase in clients opting for non-abandonment agreements. These agreements not only protect individuals but also foster a more peaceful physical separation. It's reassuring for clients to know they can start the clock on their separation without fear of abandonment claims.

Health insurance can be an issue that people worry about during separation as well. With most policies, legal separation can still allow one spouse to remain eligible for the other spouse's health insurance or other benefits, providing a degree of stability and protection during the separation period.

Once one spouse has moved out, we can then negotiate the other terms of separation. This typically involves discussing assets and liabilities (marital property division), which we refer to as **equitable distribution (ED)** in North Carolina. The law presumes that a 50/50 division is fair and equitable, so we usually start from that baseline. Part of this process is understanding the difference between **marital property** (assets and debts acquired during the marriage) and **separate property** (assets and debts that belong solely to one spouse). Those distinctions matter because they determine what goes into the division and what stays out.

It's important to understand that almost all family law matters go before a judge in North Carolina—there's no jury involved. This means a judge, who is elected by your county, will be making decisions about your finances, custody arrangements, and appropriate child support amounts.

I often tell clients that it's crucial to regain control over their decisions by engaging in **negotiations** outside of the traditional adversarial scheme of litigation. Whether working with a private mediator, going through collaborative family law, or having attorneys negotiate on their behalf, these processes empower the parties involved.

During these negotiations, we discuss several key topics: equitable distribution, which involves dividing marital assets and liabilities; spousal support, including both post-separation support and alimony; and children's issues, such as custody and support. Post-separation support is temporary spousal support, covering the period from separation to divorce, while alimony is permanent, covering the period after divorce until a future date.

Spousal support is a broad term that encompasses various forms of financial assistance from one spouse to another. For example, if one spouse moves out but continues to pay the mortgage, that can be considered in-kind spousal support. This could also apply to other bills, such as car insurance, health insurance, or household expenses. Using this blanket term allows us to reach a fair resolution regarding spousal support while considering the ability of the paying spouse to fulfill these obligations.

It's important to approach spousal support through non-litigation, as there are no specific guidelines or calculators like there are for **child support** in North Carolina. That being said, spousal support decisions tend to focus on a few main things: each spouse's income and earning potential, the lifestyle they had during the marriage, and how long they were together. Age, health, and both financial and non-financial contributions—like raising kids, supporting higher education pursuits, or furthering your spouse's career—are also considered. Ultimately, the court considers all of this to determine a fair support arrangement.

Through litigation, we need to present to the judge how we arrived at our proposed amount and why it's reasonable and fair based on these factors. Through collaborative efforts or mediation, we can work together to establish a spousal support figure that feels fair and manageable for both parties.

Property division is another significant factor in these discussions. When it comes to dividing things up in a divorce, the court considers factors different from those for spousal support. The difference is that property division is about fairly splitting what you already have, while spousal support is about ensuring one spouse isn't left without the means to move forward.

Property division can also impact spousal support. In North Carolina, if one spouse receives more than half of the net marital estate, that may affect a spousal support award or even eligibility. For instance, if someone is awarded 75 percent of the marital estate, they might not have an actual need for spousal support.

Now, you might be wondering why I mentioned no-fault divorce. There are instances in North Carolina family law where fault can play a role, which we refer to as marital misconduct. Understanding these dynamics is crucial as you navigate the complexities of divorce in North Carolina.

Marital Misconduct

Marital misconduct in North Carolina encompasses several behaviors, but is most commonly thought of as adultery. In the state's legal terminology, it's referred to as "**illicit sexual behavior**," which can sound intimidating. To break it down for clients and potential clients, I explain that illicit behavior involves any sexual act or interaction with someone outside of the marriage.

When it comes to spousal support, if a dependent spouse commits adultery, this acts as a complete bar to receiving any support. On the other hand, if the supporting spouse engages in illicit behavior, that automatically obligates them to pay alimony. While we may not know the exact amount at that moment, the analysis shifts significantly, almost like passing "Go" in a game and collecting alimony without question. This form of marital misconduct can affect spousal support, but it doesn't influence property division.

Another common factor of marital misconduct is **abandonment**, which is why non-abandonment agreements are so essential at the outset. I often clarify the difference between actual abandonment and constructive abandonment. Actual abandonment occurs when one spouse physically leaves the marital residence without notice—perhaps to start a secret life in another town. Constructive abandonment, on the other hand, involves a spouse withdrawing love and affection. For instance, if a stay-at-home parent stops cooking for the other spouse, buys groceries only for themselves, or refuses to share the same bedroom, that can be seen as constructive abandonment.

Both actual and constructive abandonment are forms of marital misconduct, and if the case goes to court, it often comes down to who the judge believes. Another example of marital misconduct is maliciously locking a spouse out of the house, which I refer to as involuntary abandonment. This occurs when one spouse changes the locks while the other is at work or out of the marital home, preventing them from entering the home when they return.

When it comes to emotional and mental abuse, it's essential to recognize that courts are increasingly weighing these forms of misconduct alongside physical abuse. In the past, emotional abuse may not have been discussed as frequently, but with more studies and an increased focus on mental health, it has gained recognition in family law. The more we talk about emotional and mental abuse, the more it is accepted as a relevant factor in spousal support cases.

Other forms of marital misconduct can include reckless spending of income by one or both spouses, concealment of income, and even the destruction of marital property. I once encountered a situation where one spouse was altering pay stubs to hide income from the other. They were directing deposits to two separate accounts and manipulating documents so that the other spouse wouldn't see the money being funneled into a secret account. This siphoning of income raises concerns about what that money is being used for—whether it's for drugs, alcohol, or other excessive expenditures to create a false perception of the marital assets and debts.

Indignities are another form of marital misconduct. This term refers to actions that render life burdensome and intolerable to the other spouse. It's more about degrading, bullying, or dehumanizing interactions rather than physical or emotional abuse. An example could be one spouse berating the other in front of coworkers at a work event, which can have significant ramifications on that person's professional reputation.

Another example of indignity might involve one spouse refusing to communicate verbally, insisting that all interactions occur in writing. This can be particularly demeaning, especially in front of children. For instance, if one spouse demands communication only via email and refuses to speak face-to-face, that behavior can be seen as an indignity in court.

Judges take these factors seriously, and sometimes I have to advise clients that collaborative law or non-litigation options may not be suitable for everyone. In unsafe scenarios where marital misconduct has occurred, I strongly recommend filing a lawsuit, as there's no way to safely rationalize or negotiate with a spouse in that environment.

Ultimately, when it comes to marital misconduct and spousal support, mediation can be a great starting point. However, my top priority is always the safety of my clients. If a situation doesn't provide a physically and emotionally safe space, I won't recommend or ask my client to engage in that process.

Proving Marital Misconduct

Proving marital misconduct can be challenging, but there are effective ways to gather evidence. Often, when it comes to adultery, clients come to me with documentation from a private investigator or their own suspicions. I work with a few trusted private investigators who know exactly how to document these situations, whether it's through pictures or videos. The level of experience may vary, but they understand what we need to prove the case.

For other types of misconduct, like reckless spending, concealment of income, or destruction of assets, things can get tricky outside of court. However, if we have a lawsuit, I can issue subpoenas, which give me access to necessary records from third parties. For example, I once handled a case where one spouse was manipulating their paychecks. By using subpoena power, we were able to access income records from their employer. This revealed a second bank account that the spouse had been hiding. By the time they provided their documents, we had already secured the subpoenaed records, making it straightforward to compare the two and uncover the truth. This illustrates how important litigation can be in cases of severe marital misconduct.

When it comes to indignities (another form of marital misconduct), it often boils down to who the judge believes. In mediation or collaborative family law settings, however, both spouses know the reality of the situation. During our collaborative four-way settlement conferences, it's challenging to hide the truth because everyone is required to disclose information fully. Failing to do so could mean starting over with a new attorney and a new process, resulting in additional time and financial expenses. This necessity for transparency in collaborative processes discourages dishonesty and promotes a more productive environment.

Some other forms of marital misconduct might be as simple as a key that works for someone who shouldn't have access or a new address that raises suspicions. We may also want to track where a spouse is spending the night. In North Carolina, it's not illegal to put trackers on cars, and many body shops know how to check for them. If a client suspects a tracker is on their vehicle, I often advise them to take the car to their local police station or sheriff's department. Leave the tracker there and inform them of their concerns about who may have placed it on their vehicle. This is a safe way to handle the situation.

Private investigators are frequently used when spousal support is in question. For example, if someone is receiving spousal support but is now living with a new partner, we can track their movements to confirm the living arrangement. Cohabitation in a romantic relationship can lead to the termination of spousal support under North Carolina law. It's important to note that simply having roommates doesn't count; it has to be a romantic partnership.

There are various ways to structure spousal support, including a specific number of payments, lump-sum payments, or a combination of both. Collaborative family law and non-litigation approaches offer flexibility in determining what works best for the parties involved. In litigation, however, they're bound by the judge's decision, which may not always align with their needs or preferences.

Is There Favoritism?

Many people believe that North Carolina law favors mothers over fathers in custody and child support cases. However, as a practitioner who has transitioned from being a student attorney to a licensed attorney, I don't find this to be true, at least not here in my local jurisdiction. That's not to say favoritism doesn't exist in other jurisdictions or counties where traditional gender roles may be more prevalent. But here, I genuinely believe there is no favoritism.

When we look at the law—specifically our North Carolina General Statutes and the case law that has come through our appellate courts—I see no evidence favoring men over women or mothers over fathers. There is, however, a significant public misconception that North Carolina is a "mother's rights" state.

If we go back a few decades, there was indeed a doctrine in family law known as the "Tender Years Doctrine." This doctrine guided custody decisions based on who was primarily responsible for child-rearing for children during their early years. The weight of custody disputes often favored that parent. Fortunately, this doctrine evolved in the late 1900s into the "best interest of the child" standard. Now, the focus is on determining what is genuinely in the child's best interest.

When litigating, I have my own approach to presenting our custody proposals to persuade the judge that our suggested arrangements serve the child's best interests. In collaborative law and non-litigation situations, we really get to the heart of what those best interests are. We prioritize the children's needs and consider what the parents have observed regarding their desires and where they will thrive the most.

For example, if one parent works the night shift, that might not be in a twelve-year-old's best interest to be left alone overnight for an entire week. We don't need a judge to tell us that. However, if we're talking about older children, like sixteen or seventeen years old, the situation could be different. A couple of hours at a time during the week, like Monday and Tuesday, might be manageable, but we must consider what kind of adult supervision is available when the child who is alone at night, is out of school, or on breaks.

Collaborative and non-litigation processes allow us to create schedules and arrangements that work best for the family, rather than adhering to a rigid schedule imposed by a judge who has only known the family for a few hours or days during trial. This flexibility is crucial for making decisions that genuinely reflect the children's needs and best interests.

The Heartbalm Torts

North Carolina is one of seven states (as of the publishing of this book) that recognize what we call **heartbalm torts**, or marital torts. The two civil claims under this category are **alienation of affection** and **criminal conversation**. Both are civil tort claims directed at a third-party defendant, rather than one spouse versus the other. In these cases, it's one spouse against a third party, typically the paramour, whether that's a mistress or another romantic interest involved with the spouse.

To establish a claim for criminal conversation, a few essential elements must be proven to a judge. First, you need to demonstrate that the marriage was a valid, intact/legal marriage between the two spouses. Second, you must demonstrate that the third-party defendant engaged in sexual relations with one of the spouses while the spouses were married. It's important to note that, despite its name, criminal conversation has nothing to do with criminal law; it simply refers to a claim regarding a married person's extramarital sexual relationship.

Alienation of affection, on the other hand, has been hotly contested and litigated through North Carolina courts. Most recently, there was a significant case in November 2025 that resulted in a million-dollar-plus judgment against a popular social media influencer. For this claim, you do not need to prove that illicit relations occurred. Instead, there are four basic elements that must be established.

1. There must be a valid legal marriage.
2. There must have been genuine love and affection in that marriage between the spouses.
3. The third party must have alienated the love and affection between the spouses.
4. But for the malicious actions of that third party, the genuine love and affection would not have been broken.

Interestingly, the third party in an alienation of affection claim can be anyone who interfered with the marriage, including a parent-in-law, an employer, or even a friend.

Many defendants in these cases have argued against the claims on constitutional grounds, citing the First Amendment right to freedom of association: the right to choose who to associate with. However, North Carolina courts have consistently rejected these arguments.

The laws in North Carolina place a high value on marriage, and I believe these claims remain in place within our state laws because of the importance our lawmakers place on maintaining the sanctity of marriage.

How It Plays Out

So, those two claims—alienation of affection and criminal conversation—can apply to anyone in a valid legal marriage, whether it's a same-sex relationship or a heterosexual marriage.

One important thing to note about these claims is the potential for recovery of damages. In the early 2010s, a multimillion-dollar judgment ($30 million in combined compensatory and punitive damages) was awarded to a spouse against her ex-husband's lover. When I counsel potential clients about these claims, I often remind them that it's going to be difficult to get blood from a turnip. Unless you have the funds to finance the process upfront and the third party has the ability to pay damages, you could end up spending a lot of money only to recover nothing. Even if you attach a lien or obtain a judgment against the third party's property, you may never see that money.

Because of this, I advise clients to approach these claims with extreme caution. Personally, I don't believe in pursuing these claims, so I won't take them on for clients. Instead, I focus on defending them and prefer to mediate rather than litigate. There are plenty of attorneys who will pursue these claims, but I've set a boundary based on my personal beliefs and values in practicing family law.

If these claims are filed in court, they typically go to the Superior Court division because they involve damages in excess of $25,000. I have seen them filed in lower district courts for amounts under $25,000, particularly in smaller, more rural counties. In those cases, some individuals have the ability to finance their claims upfront.

When a civil claim is filed in Superior Court, mediation is generally the first step before a trial. This often involves confidentiality agreements or non-disclosure agreements as part of the settlement process. Sometimes, claims are even shut down during divorce mediation when one party asks, "How much less than 50 percent are you willing to take for me not to sue your boyfriend?" It can be a strategic move to file the lawsuit, but wait to pursue it until after your divorce mediation.

In collaborative law, we prioritize full disclosure, so we don't use those tactics. However, in non-litigation scenarios, one spouse can "buy" a third-party waiver in the separation agreement. This means they might pay an additional $100,000 to include a clause stating that neither party will sue third parties for anything, specifically referring to claims of alienation of affection and criminal conversation.

When we're not in the collaborative arena, I've used this as a strategy. Sometimes, I include a third-party waiver in the initial proposed settlement document. I've had discussions shut down because the other party's attorney pointed out that their client included that waiver due to having had an affair, and they want the other spouse to give up their right to sue. This requires careful consideration of how and when to use that waiver. What began as a default clause in my draft agreements has now become something I include strategically only when it serves a specific purpose.

Third-Party Claims Timeline

The statute of limitations in North Carolina for third-party claims is three years. This went into effect in 2009 after the North Carolina General Assembly enacted N.C. Gen. Stat. §52-13. This clock starts ticking the moment you learn about the act, whether that's the act of criminal conversation between your spouse and a third party or the event that broke the love and affection in your marriage, which is relevant for alienation of affection. So, if Spouse A discovers Spouse B's affair, the day they discover this will mark the beginning of the three-year period.

Many people choose to preserve their claims by filing them and holding onto them until they reach a settlement regarding property division, alimony, child custody, or child support. With our eCourts system, fully implemented across all 100 counties of the state, it has become easier to track these claims. I can already search online for lawsuits filed against individuals in any county, and it is much simpler to find out whether someone is sitting on these types of lawsuits without having been formally served. These filings are technically public records.

You don't need to be legally separated to file third-party claims, but legal separation can help support your case for alienation of affection by demonstrating the broken love and affection in the marriage. Legal separation means living separate and apart, under two different roofs, with the intent to live as unmarried people. I often ask clients where they brush their teeth in the morning, where they make dinner, and where they sleep at night. While mail can be tricky because people can receive it anywhere, these questions help determine whether you are indeed living separate lives in two separate domiciles.

For a legal separation to occur, at least one spouse must intend to no longer live as a married couple. Once these two conditions are met, you establish your date of separation. This date is crucial because it marks when the marital estate is effectively cut off, allowing us to take a financial snapshot of everything at that moment. Any changes from the date of separation until the date of divorce are matters we actively work to resolve, whether through the courts or outside of them using collaborative law.

During this process, we evaluate various data points, such as income, to determine child support or spousal support. The timeline we often reference begins with the date of separation, which is usually the first milestone we track. People often want to know how to reach that point of separation, and once we get there, we enter a period where we work through all the outstanding issues.

Sometimes, the year-and-a-day requirement for divorce can arrive before other matters, like property division or spousal support, are resolved. Ideally, we want all these issues settled before finalizing the divorce, so that the divorce itself feels like a tidy conclusion to the business of the marriage.

I often advise clients that just as they hire a lawyer to handle the business side of their marriage, they should also seek a mental health professional to help navigate the emotional aspects. Managing these emotions is crucial, and it can be incredibly challenging without someone trained and skilled to provide support.

When to Hire a Lawyer

Knowing when to hire a lawyer can be crucial, especially if you're considering a trial separation, physical separation, or legal separation. I believe that the best time to consult an attorney is when you're starting to think about these options. It's important to understand the ramifications of legal separation and to gain a realistic view of what you need to be aware of legally.

The right time to hire me is when you've decided that you need to move out. If you feel there's no way to continue the relationship while living in the same household, that's when we should talk. At this point, we can explore various options, like sending a demand letter or making a formal request. If your spouse has an attorney, I can reach out to them as well.

In North Carolina, we have what is called a **Divorce from Bed and Board**. It sounds like a divorce, but it doesn't actually break the bonds of matrimony. Instead, it's essentially a court-ordered legal separation. The court can order one spouse to move out, which is important if someone refuses to leave the shared home. If you find yourself in that situation—where your spouse can't afford the house but won't vacate—that's the point when you should hire me.

I will make a good-faith effort to encourage your spouse to leave, and try to resolve the issue without escalating it to litigation. However, if that doesn't work and they still refuse to move out, we can file a lawsuit for divorce from bed and board to enforce that legal separation.

> It's important to note that pursuing this legal route doesn't mean we can't work through other issues without further litigation. We can still negotiate and resolve matters amicably, but sometimes you need that legal action to get the ball rolling and ensure that your spouse moves out, starting the clock on the separation process.

The Safeguard State

I definitely believe that North Carolina has a wealth of laws and subsequent case law that provide safeguards to protect individuals who have been wronged. This protection isn't about being malicious or seeking revenge; it's more about helping the aggrieved spouse—let's call them the wronged spouse—become whole again. The focus is on restitution rather than punishment.

In this context, alienation of affection and criminal conversation claims can feel quite punitive. They take a more extreme adversarial approach, which can exacerbate tensions. However, there are still ways to resolve these issues without escalating to full-blown litigation. Often, such claims begin with demand letters, cease-and-desist notices, or requests to stop all interactions. You might see something like, "I demand that you cease this behavior and pay me $5 million to prevent me from suing you."

Fortunately, many of these disputes can be settled through pre-litigation mediation or arbitration. North Carolina has established various avenues to assist those who feel they have been wronged, allowing for resolution without necessarily resorting to punitive measures. The goal is to create a system that aims to restore rather than retaliate, ensuring that people have the support they need to move forward.

Domestic Violence Protective Orders

When domestic violence is an issue in the Tar Heel State, we refer to protective orders as **50Bs**, named after the chapter in the general statutes that govern these issues. These orders function similarly to restraining orders, typically issued when a spouse or romantic partner has abused the other. However, the definition has expanded to include individuals in romantic relationships, regardless of whether or not they currently live together.

A few years ago, an attorney argued a case that made its way through the North Carolina Supreme Court, which affirmed that protective orders also apply to same-sex relationships. This was a significant development because, prior to this ruling, there was no recourse for domestic violence in same-sex relationships, despite the fact that these relationships share many of the same dynamics as heterosexual relationships.

Whenever I see allegations of domestic violence or filings related to it, I always advise my clients about collaborative law. It's crucial to discuss feelings, emotions, and needs, particularly with respect to safety. We must ask questions like: Do you feel safe being in the same room as the other person? Would you feel safe even being on a Zoom call with them? More often than not, the answer is no. When clients express that they don't feel safe or don't want to be vulnerable around their partner, I suggest that they consider having the other party retain a lawyer so that I can negotiate on their behalf. If that doesn't work, we may need to file a lawsuit.

Mediation is always an option before heading to court. Judges in North Carolina appreciate it when parties attempt this option. In mediation, the parties are typically in separate rooms, often with multiple doors between them. This allows for a safer environment while still providing the protection of the court.

If someone is threatening you—such as cornering you in a parking lot or following you—there are steps you can take to protect yourself. At the courthouse, while it can feel intimidating, sheriff's deputies and security personnel are present, adding another layer of protection. In litigation cases involving domestic violence, I take extra precautions for my clients. I might have them wait in a witness room rather than in the courtroom, or sit in a different hallway, if I know the other party is present.

Physical and emotional safety is paramount when we discuss litigation. I also counsel clients on financial matters, especially when there are allegations of financial misconduct. I explain that litigation can provide the tools we need to obtain what they won't give us voluntarily. However, it's essential to note that we can still resolve matters outside of a lengthy trial.

In North Carolina, we have judicial settlement conferences where parties and their attorneys can meet with a judge to help resolve disputes. The judge acts somewhat like a mediator, but won't be the presiding judge if the case goes to trial. There are always options available. It's common for judges on the day of trial to encourage attorneys to step into a meeting room to see if they can work things out. They often ask us to forecast our evidence, which allows them to unofficially forecast how they might lean in their ruling.

I wouldn't say they tell us how they will rule, but they definitely encourage attorneys and parties to find resolutions to avoid lengthy trials. When considering basic property divisions or spousal support cases, you can expect these to take anywhere from four to six months just to reach court-ordered mediation. Custody cases may take longer, generally around nine to twelve months, before reaching a trial date.

As you can see, the legal landscape provides numerous routes to safety and resolution, and choosing and navigating these options requires knowledge about each and careful consideration. You don't want to go it alone.

In this chapter, we talked about North Carolina's rules—what triggers the separation clock, what can reset it, what a judge can decide, and what litigation can cost you emotionally and financially.

The next question is whether you really want a judge who knows nothing about you making the most personal decisions of your life. That's where Chapter 2 begins.

Collaborative family law is an alternative for people who still need structure and protection but want to trade the courtroom battlefield for a process built on privacy, full disclosure, and problem-solving.

CHAPTER 2

The Collaborative Family Law Framework

Collaborative family law, which I often refer to simply as collaborative law, has two key principles. First, parties agree not to litigate. This doesn't mean legal proceedings are entirely off the table. For instance, filing what I call a "**friendly lawsuit**" might be necessary to get a court order to divide a retirement account. But the general commitment is to avoid litigation. Second, if anyone decides to withdraw from the collaborative process, they must provide written notice to all parties and to the attorneys involved. Also, the attorneys who represented you in the collaborative process cannot represent you in any adversarial litigation.

At the beginning of the process, everyone involved signs a **collaborative pledge**. It's a contract that outlines these commitments. The main objectives of this pledge are to:

- Agree to keep **collaborative law proceedings** private.
- Agree not to litigate in court.
- Agree to maintain full disclosure throughout the process.

This means there won't be any surprises or last-minute revelations; everything is laid out from the start.

In terms of communication, I advocate for nonviolent communication and use an **interest-based negotiation model** rather than focusing solely on outcomes. This approach, originally developed by Marshall B. Rosenberg, PhD, enables open and honest discussions and involves what we call four-way settlement conferences, where all parties come together to resolve issues. Communication between meetings is transparent, involving all parties and their attorneys, thereby supporting full disclosure.

This method helps an individual focus on their own needs while also considering the needs and interests of their former partners. I break down the communication process into four parts: observe, feel, need, request (OFNR). For example, I might say, "Susie, I see that you are sighing heavily, and it seems you're feeling frustrated. Would you like to share a need, and then perhaps make a request based on that?"

Using this structured method of communication not only helps us reach peaceful outcomes but also fosters long-term personal growth. Once you learn it, you can use it to improve your relationships with children, co-parents, or your parents, as it becomes a natural part of how you interact; it extends beyond the immediate situation.

I also provide clients with tools such as worksheets or cheat sheets to help them practice effective communication. These tools are simple yet effective, with spaces to formulate and fill in straightforward statements.

During one memorable session, I watched these tools really do their job. It was a challenging situation with one person who was particularly aggressive and not at all mindful of their language. Thanks to the structured communication method, the other collaborative attorney and I were able to steer the conversation back on track and continue the meeting. However, it definitely made it clear that there would be an ongoing need for guidance in nonviolent communication for this particular group.

This is why I emphasize a collaborative approach, especially in contrast with the adversarial nature of traditional court proceedings, where the two parties often feel pitted against each other from the start. Collaborative law not only resolves issues more quickly but also keeps personal matters private, which is increasingly important as more court systems, like ours in North Carolina, move to electronic filing, where records are readily accessible to anyone with internet access.

We spend our first meeting discussing the collaborative process and the communication methods we'll use, rather than diving straight into the legal issues. This sets the stage for the entire process, ensuring everyone understands and agrees on the approach before moving forward. This way, we avoid wasting time and resources if the collaborative method isn't suitable for everyone involved.

What is Collaborative Family Law

Essentially, collaborative family law is a form of alternative dispute resolution, recognized in various jurisdictions, including North Carolina. Over five years ago, North Carolina adopted the Uniform Civil Collaborative Law Act, legally recognizing it under our general statutes as a valid means of settling disputes outside traditional court litigation.

So, what does alternative dispute resolution entail? It offers different ways and formats for resolving legal disputes without going to court. This can range from arbitration, where a neutral arbitrator acts similarly to a judge but within set parameters, to more personal negotiations involving just the disputing parties and their attorneys.

> Collaborative family law is a unique option within alternative dispute resolution. It involves both parties actively participating in the resolution process to preserve their long-term emotional, financial, and mental health and that of their families.

This method is distinguished by a few key features. The first is that all parties and their attorneys sign the collaborative pledge I mentioned earlier. This agreement outlines how everyone agrees to proceed, emphasizing full disclosure and the potential use of third-party, **collaborative neutrals** such as appraisers, forensic accountants, or child welfare specialists to assist in resolving the dispute.

I often describe collaborative family law as a way to resolve family disagreements—whether they're about finances, legal separation, or child custody—through cooperation rather than conflict. It's a method that allows both parties to sit together, whether in person or virtually, to express their needs and listen actively to one another.

The tools available to collaborative practitioners are varied, enabling them to facilitate discussions that help both parties reach a common ground and create long-lasting solutions. I believe that collaborative family law works best when people are able to look beyond their immediate emotions, communicate effectively, and remain open to the process with the support of their attorneys.

While no family dispute is ideal, the collaborative process offers a constructive and respectful way to resolve issues, making it a valuable option for those willing to work together toward a mutually beneficial outcome.

The Collaborative Pledge

The Collaborative Pledge, which some refer to as a promise or agreement, is akin to an honor pledge. Growing up, I attended a small private school where the honor system was highly valued. It promoted fairness and peace, ensuring everyone worked towards their goals with integrity and adhered to principles such as not cheating, stealing, or lying.

Similarly, the collaborative pledge in family law is intended to uphold a high standard of conduct throughout the legal process. From first grade through college and even law school, I was required to sign an honor pledge for every test, quiz, and assignment, reinforcing the importance of these values. This pledge was so ingrained in me that

I remember a specific incident in sixth grade where I repeatedly (but accidentally) misspelled 'received' and had to write it correctly dozens of times as a consequence. Pledges like these have had a deep impact on my academic life and beyond.

In collaborative family law, the pledge serves as the foundational agreement on how the parties will conduct themselves. It includes commitments to full disclosure and respectful treatment of all involved. Parties agree to use an interest-based model of negotiation rather than a positional model and commit to other specific actions or inactions, such as agreeing not to litigate. If the process must be terminated, it requires written notice from all parties and their attorneys, and the collaborative attorneys may not thereafter represent the clients in litigation.

This pledge is not just a formality but is required by statute and is a vital part of the collaborative process because it's there to ensure that all **collaborative participants** come to the table with a shared understanding and commitment. It's about creating a safe and supportive environment where everyone is on the same team, not opposing sides.

Additionally, certain legal requirements, such as transferring retirement account funds, may necessitate what we call 'friendly lawsuits.' These are exceptions within the collaborative framework where legal actions are required by law but are carried out in the spirit of the collaborative pledge.

Full disclosure is a crucial part of this pledge. It ensures that no information is withheld and that all cards are on the table from the start. This transparency is so important for building trust among parties and laying the foundation for equitable solutions. For example, if one person gets a new job, updated income information must be shared promptly.

We strive to make sure that all discussions and negotiations are conducted openly and respectfully, aligning with the collaborative law's goal of resolving family disputes amicably and equitably.

For the Kids

I believe that collaborative family law is better for kids. When I speak to potential clients, I often share with them how much control they retain over how and when they see their children when they choose this route. Unlike in the court system, where a judge, who is essentially a stranger, dictates your parenting decisions, collaborative law empowers parents to devise their own co-parenting plans.

This is especially helpful for younger children, including those in elementary school. For these kids, it can be incredibly challenging to go more than two or three days without seeing one of their parents. I always advocate for arrangements that keep both parents actively involved in their young children's lives as frequently as possible.

For instance, while some parents might opt for alternating weeks, this schedule might not suit everyone, especially if the children are not yet in school. I had one client who successfully arranged a two-week-on, two-weeks-off schedule until their child started school because one parent lived outside of North Carolina, and it worked for their families.

In essence, collaborative family law places the decision-making power back into the hands of the parents, allowing them to tailor parenting plans that best suit their family's unique needs and circumstances. This approach not only fosters a better parenting environment but also significantly benefits the children involved.

Friendly Lawsuits

A friendly lawsuit might sound like a contradiction, but it's actually a practical tool within family law. Take matters like **child support** and **child custody**. Typically, these can be resolved through private agreements such as parenting plans or a separation agreement that includes property division. These agreements allow parents to maintain privacy while outlining the terms of parenting and support.

However, there are situations where involving the court can be beneficial or even necessary. For example, some individuals prefer that child support payments be deducted directly from their paychecks, which requires a formal court order. This method can be particularly appealing if direct financial interactions between ex-partners are stressful or uncomfortable. In such cases, we might include the agreed-upon child support terms into a consent court order, which a judge then signs off on. This legal step enables the initiation of income withholding, so the child support payments are transferred directly from one parent's employer to the other, minimizing direct contact between the two.

This process often proves useful, especially in situations where we're working to repair co-parenting relationships or when direct interactions between parents have been problematic. If needed, we can create a court-adopted parenting agreement or a child support agreement that becomes part of the divorce judgment. By incorporating these private agreements into a divorce judgment, they gain the enforceability of a court order.

Another scenario where a friendly lawsuit might be necessary is in the division of retirement funds, which legally requires a court order to transfer. Here again, we can include the necessary provisions in a divorce judgment, which then facilitates the execution of these agreements through legal channels.

Despite the name, a friendly lawsuit isn't about conflict. Instead, it's a cooperative approach where all parties agree to involve the court to formalize certain aspects of their agreements, ensuring they are legally binding and can be implemented effectively. This method combines the privacy and flexibility of private contracts with the enforceability of a court order, offering a balanced solution in sensitive family law matters.

Choosing Collaborative Family Law

The most compelling reasons to opt for collaborative family law center around protecting your financial health, emotional well-being, mental health, and the quality of your relationships. These four aspects are vital to your long-term happiness and how you envision your future unfolding. In my experience, these are the primary benefits people experience, even though they tend to recognize these advantages only after the process has concluded.

If you are concerned about the cost of engaging a lawyer and navigating the court system, and the financial burden that can become, you are certainly not alone. Many people fear the uncertainty of expenses, the potential need to borrow money, or even going into debt. The duration of traditional legal proceedings can inflate these costs, as time taken off work for court appearances adds up. Collaborative family law, however, generally involves less expense than litigation. This is not just in terms of attorney fees; the process itself is designed to be more flexible and less burdensome financially.

Collaborative law offers greater control over your decisions compared to a court-dictated process, especially when discussing child support, spousal support, and the division of marital assets. For instance, deciding between a lump-sum payment as opposed to monthly spousal support can significantly impact both parties' financial health and emotional state. In collaborative settings, these issues are navigated with a focus on the long-term needs and goals of everyone involved.

From the beginning, we discuss your financial objectives and identify potential stressors. Conversations might explore scenarios like achieving an ideal retirement age or adjusting support structures to accommodate future needs. While it's not always possible to meet everyone's goals perfectly, through the collaborative process, we are often successful in crafting agreements that respect each party's priorities and limitations.

> Ultimately, choosing collaborative family law means opting for a process that considers the whole person and their broader life context, not just the immediate legal issues. This holistic approach can help reduce the emotional and financial strain that often accompanies family law disputes.

Preserving Emotional Health

Collaborative family law is particularly effective in safeguarding long-term emotional health, especially when compared with traditional litigation, which is adversarial right from the get-go. In North Carolina, for instance, the initial lawsuit papers starkly announce that a lawsuit has been filed against you, often punctuated with exclamation points. This approach can feel so confrontational and stressful.

In contrast, collaborative family law adopts a more conciliatory approach. We gather around the table—literally and figuratively—to discuss and resolve issues. In our practice, we even prefer rounded tables instead of square ones to emphasize the non-adversarial nature of the process. It's a subtle yet powerful way to signal that everyone is on the same team, rather than opposing sides. This setup helps reduce the feelings of defensiveness and attack that are often associated with litigation.

The use of nonviolent communication also helps to preserve emotional well-being because it removes the adversarial element from the proceedings. By doing so, we shift the mindset from a combative "you versus me" to a collaborative "us together." This change in perspective eliminates the need to fight over who files first or the stigma of being the defendant.

Ultimately, collaborative family law focuses on reducing the heightened emotions and overwhelm that typically accompany legal disputes. By fostering a team-oriented atmosphere, we help protect your emotional well-being throughout the process, making it not just a legal resolution but a holistic one.

Preserving Long-Term Mental Health

I want to distinguish mental health from emotional health here. Emotional health often refers to immediate stressors, such as worrying about who will pay the mortgage if one person moves out. These are day-to-day concerns that impact how you feel and interact in the moment. Mental health, on the other hand, involves deeper, long-standing issues that might have been part of the relationship dynamics for years, such as hidden financial troubles or deceit.

For instance, consider a long-term marriage where one spouse was the primary breadwinner while the other managed the household and children. If financial issues were concealed from the spouse who didn't work outside the home, this could lead to significant mental strain and trauma. In collaborative law, addressing these issues might involve separate discussions with each spouse in different rooms (**collaborative caucuses**) before everyone feels comfortable coming together at the collaborative table.

There might be cases of anger or other strong emotions that need to be managed carefully throughout the process. Ensuring safety, both emotionally and physically, is paramount. This safety is extended not only to the clients but also to their attorneys and any other professionals involved. Regular debriefs with clients, attorneys, and neutral parties help maintain this safe environment.

In my collaborative practice, our clients' mental health is a priority. Unlike traditional litigation, which often focuses solely on legal disputes, collaborative law considers the overall well-being of the entire family. This approach is crucial, especially in cases involving the dissolution, separation, or division of a family. We take into account any trauma, long-term stress, or emotional fallout that may have occurred during the marriage or partnership. We don't just address the immediate issues; we also consider the long-term mental health of everyone involved. This might mean bringing in child welfare specialists, licensed clinical social workers, psychologists, or psychiatrists who are trained in collaborative practices. These professionals help ensure that the mental health of all parties is addressed, not just during the proceedings but in the long term. Throughout the process, our overall goal is to protect and enhance the mental health of all involved, creating a foundation for healthier, long-term interactions.

Safety is Important

Safety is a cornerstone of collaborative family law. We strive to ensure that all parties involved, including attorneys, clients, and children, feel secure throughout the process. This is essential not only for emotional and mental well-being but also for achieving a meaningful resolution. Whether the concerns stem from trauma experienced during the relationship or challenges in co-parenting, promoting a sense of safety is paramount.

Physical safety is equally important. In cases where there is a history of domestic violence or even a concern regarding potential violence, I typically do not recommend collaborative family law. However, there are exceptions if the parties feel secure. If my client feels safer not being in the same physical space as the other party, we can facilitate their participation via a Zoom call. This allows them to engage in the process without the need to be physically present, which can help in maintaining safety.

This approach also helps keep the process private, which is particularly important given the public nature of courtrooms and the shift toward more publicly accessible electronic court systems, like North Carolina's **eCourts**. By keeping these matters out of the traditional court setting, we can avoid the trauma of reliving painful experiences in a public forum and protect the individual's privacy. We want to ensure that everyone involved can participate fully and openly without fear.

Relationship Health

In my practice, whether it involves a law case or managing client relationships, my focus is always on the long term. While it is essential to meet immediate goals and outcomes related to emotional, financial, and mental health, maintaining healthy relationships is vital, especially when children are involved. In family law disputes involving children, it's almost certain that you'll have ongoing interactions with your co-parent due to shared events like birthdays, graduations, and other significant life moments.

Many people caught in the throes of family law issues tend to focus on immediate concerns:

- How much will I need to pay in child support?
- How can I ensure the other party pays the court-ordered spousal support?
- Who gets to keep the house?

These are common questions that arise, but it's crucial to remember that the other party may very well be a part of your life indefinitely.

In collaborative family law, we have the opportunity to remove the adversarial aspect often seen in litigation. This shift gives you the ability to maintain healthy relationships with your co-parent or former partner, even when new partners are introduced into the family dynamic. Whether it's navigating the introduction of a new partner to children or unraveling financial ties in a marriage, the goal is always to consider the long-term impacts alongside immediate needs.

When you hold onto trauma and stress, it can hinder your ability to move on or enter into new relationships. It's important, therefore, to not just focus on the "now," like the specific terms of a resolution, but also on the long-term health of all relationships involved. This perspective is something I find lacking in traditional litigation, where the focus is predominantly on achieving immediate client goals without considering the long-term implications.

In collaborative law, especially in family settings, we're trained to think about the future. We consider how today's decisions will impact our clients after three, five, or even fifteen years. This foresight comes from experience and understanding the dynamics of family relationships over time. For example, when I primarily handled litigated cases, the focus was on immediate wins, such as securing physical custody or decision-making rights. But as I shifted toward a more collaborative approach, I recognized the value in considering the long-term outcomes of these decisions.

We also prepare for future changes. Our agreements include provisions for potential disagreements or adjustments down the line, ensuring the collaborative process continues to provide a framework for resolution. This gives clients peace of mind, knowing that if issues arise years later, they still have a supportive structure to return to, avoiding the need for court interventions.

By focusing on both immediate and long-term outcomes, collaborative family law not only addresses current legal needs but also fosters a healthier, more sustainable environment for all parties involved, particularly for children, so future challenges can be managed cooperatively and respectfully.

My Training in Collaborative Family Law

Let's delve into the training recommended for collaborative family law. Collaborative civil law, which includes family law because it's a civil matter, generally involves disputes between individuals or entities, whether person vs. person or business owner vs. business owner.

In the realm of collaborative law, practitioners are encouraged to complete at least an initial fourteen-hour **civil collaborative law training** program. I underwent this comprehensive training over two days at the start of 2019. Following this, it's recommended that practitioners engage in additional training (typically six to eight hours annually) to keep their skills sharp and to continue adding new tools and techniques to their repertoire. These sessions are crucial for learning from other experienced practitioners in North Carolina and beyond.

While this ongoing education isn't mandatory, it is highly recommended. Most family law collaborative attorneys voluntarily adhere to this practice because it significantly enhances their ability to serve their clients effectively. This training helps them focus on key aspects such as ensuring clients feel safe and addressing their financial, emotional, mental, and relational health.

The training recalibrates and enriches our approach as attorneys, enabling us to meet the diverse needs of our clients more effectively. Whether it's addressing alimony, child support, or ensuring a separated spouse and children have what they need for a stable, healthy life, our training continually brings us back to the core of why we do what we do. It's about honing existing skills and acquiring new ones to better facilitate the collaborative process and achieve the best possible outcomes for everyone involved.

Transforming How People Break Up

I firmly believe that collaborative law can revolutionize the way people handle breakups or separations. Traditionally, ending relationships can be abrupt and filled with conflict, leading to behaviors like changing locks while the other person is at work or on a trip. These behaviors not only escalate conflict but also leave lasting emotional scars.

Collaborative family law offers a more peaceful, much more respectful alternative to these conventional confrontations. As this approach becomes better known and more mainstream, though it varies by region, it could significantly change the landscape of family law.

Just today, as I was working on this chapter, a colleague from another legal practice area asked me about training in collaborative family law. I had to explain that developing this type of practice takes time. It has taken me over seven years to refine my skills and continually educate myself to better serve my clients.

The more legal professionals adopt this approach, the more common it will become, therefore potentially overhauling the family law field in places like North Carolina and beyond. This shift could change not only how legal professionals operate but also how individuals choose to end their relationships, whether romantic or co-parenting. My goal is always to create a process that supports everyone involved to transition more smoothly and respectfully, which I believe is achievable with more widespread adoption of collaborative family law.

In this chapter, we discussed the collaborative process and how it doesn't avoid conflict; it can avoid rushing into battle. It's a communication system that keeps discussions respectful and focused on resolution. But once you accept the framework, what determines whether it works? For instance, how are you going to talk to each other when it gets hard?

In Chapter 3, we move from the structure of collaboration to the skill that makes it usable: Nonviolent communication—a practical method for saying what you mean, hearing what's being said, and working through emotional landmines without stepping on them.

CHAPTER 3

Nonviolent Communication in Practice

In collaborative family law, how we speak to one another matters. Clear communication is really the only way to reach a resolution. To do that, we use what's called nonviolent communication (NVC). Essentially, it's a way to interact with others that removes aggression and emotionally charged language. For instance, consider the phrase "I don't hate you that much." This might not explicitly say "I hate you a lot," but that's obviously the underlying message you would hear. Nonviolent communication aims to eliminate such undertones.

Here's how NVC works in practice: Let's say in a meeting, I'm dealing with someone like Susie, whose attorney is also present. If Susie makes a statement that could be perceived as aggressive, I might ask her, "Can you phrase that as a request?" or "Can you share what you're observing, what you're feeling, and what you need?" This approach helps clarify the communication.

Because it is often difficult for parties to change the way they communicate with each other (for example, passive-aggressive texts flying back and forth), I suggest that all communications be limited to email among the four of us on the collaborative team—both parties and their attorneys—to support transparency as part of the collaborative process. This method ensures transparency and helps us move forward, even if only with small resolutions at each meeting. Since I made that shift, this approach has proven effective.

Nonviolent communication, especially when written, requires us to be formulaic in our interactions, stripping away unwritten emotions. In one sentence, nonviolent communication is about articulating our needs and feelings without hidden aggression or emotional triggers.

An Important Tool

NVC is one of our most pivotal tools in the collaborative law process, applicable to various civil collaborative law scenarios, including family businesses, general business dealings, construction, and civil litigation disputes. However, it's particularly significant in family law. This method, developed by Marshall B. Rosenberg, Ph.D. (author of *Nonviolent Communication: A Language of Life*), focuses on fostering compassion rather than domination—a fundamental principle in collaborative family law.

In collaborative settings, the typical adversarial approach is replaced with compassion. This shift profoundly changes the dynamic, allowing participants to see beyond themselves and engage more freely, with fewer concerns about self-protection. It encourages active listening and protects each party's vulnerability while enabling open communication about needs and requests.

From the outset of client relationships, I introduce NVC. During initial consultations where I sense collaborative family law is appropriate, I share its importance. Once clients retain me, we delve deeper in preparation meetings, especially before our first four-way settlement conference. I emphasize that mastering NVC requires practice; it's not an overnight skill, especially when past interactions may have been marked by discord or hurt feelings.

Throughout the collaborative process, whether in four-way meetings or one-on-one caucuses, I consistently apply NVC. And it isn't just a useful tool professionally; I've applied it within my own family dynamics. As a first-generation American with immigrant parents from India, blending Eastern and Western values, I've found NVC instrumental in navigating cultural and personal communications, protecting myself from potential hurt while fostering understanding.

We begin our settlement conferences by addressing the immediate concerns of all parties involved, using NVC to frame these discussions. For instance, if a breadwinner learns they are about to be laid off, we discuss this openly, focusing on expressing and addressing the underlying needs and feelings associated with such significant life changes. This approach not only helps in articulating difficult messages but also in receiving them, which can be transformative for all parties involved.

NVC isn't just a technique; it's a lifestyle change that I hope clients will continue to apply beyond the collaborative process, whether in professional settings or personal relationships. It's a powerful tool for hearing and sharing difficult messages. In four-way settlement conferences, we not only pledge to collaborate but also engage with NVC to ensure that everyone's voice is heard and their needs are considered, setting the stage for a constructive and compassionate dialogue right from the start.

The Elements of Nonviolent Communication

Let's delve into the core elements of NVC, starting with observations. The key distinction here is between simple observations and evaluations. We aim to remove judgment and opinion statements and focus purely on what is directly observable. Questions like "What do I see? What do I hear?" help us stick to the facts without infusing personal interpretations.

For instance, think of a scenario involving child support. An observation might be, "I see that you put half the amount into the account for our children's expenses compared to last month." This is a straightforward statement. An evaluation, however, adds a layer of interpretation, such as, "I see you only put half the amount because you don't think we need it." This introduces assumptions and can lead to misunderstandings.

The power of sticking to pure observations lies in its ability to foster open communication and active listening. When evaluations slip in, they tend to make the listener defensive, which can shut down effective dialogue. You might even see physical signs of someone closing off, like leaning back or crossing their arms. I've seen how such statements turn off the listener from being receptive to the message in our four-way conferences, and this is where an experienced collaborative attorney can help reframe the statements and message through NVC.

Moving beyond verbal communication, NVC also encompasses nonverbal cues that can significantly influence the dynamics of a settlement conference. If I notice nonverbal signs of closure, I might suggest a brief caucus, where each party can regroup separately with their attorneys before reconvening. This allows everyone a moment to process and return to the discussion more open and ready to engage.

The next element of NVC is feelings. We differentiate actual feelings from thoughts about those feelings. For example, instead of saying, "I feel uneasy because you are not meeting my needs," you might simply state, "I feel uneasy." This approach avoids mixing feelings with accusatory or assumptive language.

Then, we address needs. Clearly stating needs without implying blame on anyone is crucial. Continuing with the child support example, you might express, "I have a need for financial security to pay my bills." This clearly communicates the need without attributing motives to the other party's actions.

By using the elements of clear observations, expressed feelings, and stated needs, we can break down potentially domineering statements into constructive dialogue. This approach fosters understanding and cooperation, rather than escalating conflict and stress. It shifts the focus from confrontation to finding mutually agreeable solutions, potentially saving time, reducing legal costs, and most importantly, preserving relationships.

NVC in Action

The theory of NVC is simplified by Marshall B. Rosenberg into four essential elements in my practice.

1. Observing
2. Feelings
3. Needs
4. Requests

I even keep a laminated hot pink sticky note with these terms on my desk to ensure they're always at the forefront of my mind, whether I'm engaging in virtual meetings, in-person sessions, or phone calls.

During the initial collaborative session, alongside the other collaborative attorney, we decide on the handouts or documents we'll use to guide our clients through the NVC process. One of the most important is the *feelings and needs worksheet*, which serves as an inventory list to help clients familiarize themselves with using this formulaic way of communication.

The process begins by focusing solely on factual experiences without judgment or labels. For example, imagine you are a separated spouse in a settlement conference. You've been a stay-at-home parent throughout your twenty-year marriage, and your spouse, the breadwinner, states they will no longer deposit money into the joint account because of unspecified spending concerns. Using NVC, your response would be grounded in observation: "When I hear you say you won't contribute more money to the account, I feel uneasy because I need financial support to pay bills for myself and the children."

This leads us to feelings, where we express emotional responses without embedding thoughts, using straightforward feeling words like calm, frustrated, or hopeful. We differentiate these based on whether:

- They feel their needs are met or not.
- It feels joyful or calm when the needs are met.
- It feels uneasy or scary when needs are not met.

Next, we discuss needs. These are fundamental human desires, including autonomy, honesty, respect, and being valued as a partner. It's crucial to articulate these needs without linking them to monetary contributions, and to emphasize the emotional and practical contributions within the household.

Finally, we address requests. These are expressed without expecting a specific outcome, differentiating them from demands. For example, instead of demanding, "I need you to put $5,000 into my bank account monthly," you would request, "Would you consider setting up a monthly transfer to help cover our bills?"

This method requires practice and doesn't yield immediate results. Throughout the collaborative process, I provide cheat sheets and, in virtual settings, drop helpful hints in the chat to help everyone adopt this communication style. Over time, this fosters a resolution-focused discussion that preserves peace and relationships.

For instance, I worked with a couple, both with advanced degrees, where one had chosen to stay home with the children. This arrangement led to feelings of being undervalued and perceived only as a financial provider. It took multiple sessions and careful reframing of communication to shift the focus from financial contributions to recognizing each person's needs and contributions.

> Trust between collaborative attorneys is crucial. We often help each other's clients reframe their statements from mere observations to expressions of needs and requests. This approach prevents adversarial breakdowns and focuses on understanding and addressing the interests of each party.

In one case, I observed that one spouse wasn't fully grasping the concept of NVC, appearing to have a results-based mindset. Recognizing this early, I discussed a strategy with their collaborative attorney to better integrate NVC into our discussions, with the aim of achieving meaningful progress in our next meetings. This approach ensures that both parties feel seen, heard, and safe, making NVC one of the most potent tools in my toolbox as a collaborative family law attorney.

In another situation that started out with very heavy feelings, there was a stay-at-home spouse who had left a medical career to raise the family and work inside the home, while the other spouse, also a professional, worked outside the home during the entirety of the marriage. The spouse who gave up their career felt very unappreciated and unheard.

At the very beginning of the collaborative process, I could see that those feelings were a big wall, blocking us from moving forward. We couldn't even begin to break down the issues or talk about how property would be divided until we got past that. We needed to look at everyone's budget, the family's cash flow, and then brainstorm solutions and options they could choose from that would meet most, if not all, of their needs.

Nonviolent Communication was such a powerful tool there. It didn't mean ignoring or burying emotions. It meant creating a way for both spouses to open up. I think it worked because the other collaborative attorney and I used nonviolent communication with each other in their presence during our four-way sessions.

After our first session (which was virtual, not our preference at the time), we debriefed together. Then, once we had our first in-person session, we tried something that worked really well: I would echo and reframe what the other spouse (not my client) had said, using nonviolent communication, and the other collaborative attorney would do the same with my client.

This approach helped both spouses begin to break down those walls. It reminded everyone of the bigger purpose—why we were there in the first place. And keeping nonviolent communication in our toolbox throughout the process really helped everyone be more open, more receptive, and more willing to work toward a resolution that met their needs.

Four-way Settlement Conferences

Four-way settlement conferences often resemble therapy sessions. When explaining this to my clients, I sometimes point to my law license hanging in my office, which labels me as both an attorney and a Counselor. This serves as a reminder that our role extends beyond legal duties; we are also committed to our clients' well-being.

These meetings can be quite intense. Recognizing this, I emphasize the importance of debriefing and decompressing afterwards. Personally, I find these sessions emotionally taxing, so I have a rule against scheduling two four-way conferences back-to-back, and I limit the number I conduct in a day to ensure I have adequate time to reset.

For clients, the emotional toll is significant. I often advise them to seek mental health support and recommend scheduling therapy sessions post-conference to provide a safe space for decompression. Depending on our schedules, I arrange debriefs with clients either immediately following the session or the next day. This timing allows them to engage in activities that help distance them from the intensity of the conference, such as taking a walk or watching a light-hearted TV show, providing a mental break and helping clear their minds.

Adopting nonviolent communication within this framework can be profoundly healing. It not only assists clients during this challenging phase but also equips them with tools for healthier communication in the future.

A Safe Space

Creating a safe space during four-way settlement conferences is incredibly important. I recall a situation where a separated spouse, not my client, felt ganged up on. This was deeply concerning to me as it is never my intention to make anyone feel unsafe or attacked. I discussed this with their collaborative attorney to determine how I could better ensure a sense of safety. It's essential to remember that, despite our intentions, what truly matters is how our communication is received. This situation was a strong reminder to always be mindful of how others are interpreting our words and to strive for a safe environment where everyone feels they are on equal footing, and working toward a common goal.

As a collaborative attorney, I believe it is my duty to ensure that our conferences are perceived as safe spaces. This starts with how we organize and plan our meetings. We make a point of structuring the sessions so that everyone has a turn to speak without feeling overshadowed. At the start of each meeting, we revisit the communication tools we will use, which sets the tone for respectful and balanced dialogue.

Still, maintaining this environment requires constant vigilance, which can be mentally taxing for the attorneys involved. It's part of our role to monitor the conversation closely and intervene if it deviates from nonviolent communication. If I detect any adversarial statements or if the discourse escalates, I won't hesitate to call for a break. This could mean taking a moment for a private caucus with our clients, stepping outside for a brief discussion among attorneys, or even pausing for a refreshment break. These pauses help everyone do a reset.

For example, in one challenging session, simply taking a five-minute break for a drink and a quick walk helped realign everyone involved. Whether it's stretching our legs, hydrating, or grabbing a quick coffee, these small actions can make a big difference.

I regularly use these strategies, even outside of collaborative settings, to ensure my work environment is a safe space. Whether it's stepping away from my desk for a brief walk or taking a moment to regroup, these practices help manage mental exhaustion and maintain a secure, productive environment for all participants in the collaborative process. Sessions become more effective, and participants are encouraged to remain engaged and feel valued throughout.

Tracking Resolutions

I have yet to see a collaborative case end without a resolution, but it can happen. When the process weighs on my client's mental health, it is important that they have an outlet to help manage their mental well-being throughout the collaborative process. These issues do impact our process, which is why I opt for additional debriefing sessions with my fellow collaborative attorney and my client. Our goal is to ensure that if our clients are unable to articulate certain issues themselves, we can still create a safe environment for them. Sometimes, it requires us attorneys to provide more hands-on guidance throughout the process.

Dealing with challenging personality types, especially in cases that might involve narcissistic traits, is tricky. I'm cautious about using terms like "narcissist" or "gaslighting", or even "alienation," words that I find are often overused in family law. I prefer to reserve these labels for situations where a mental health professional has provided a specific diagnosis. After fifteen years in the field as a student attorney and a practicing attorney, I trust my ability to understand these complex behaviors, though I always try to approach each case with an open mind.

For instance, it's not uncommon for one party to accuse the other of gaslighting during litigation. However, upon reviewing the written communications, it's often clear that what's being labeled as gaslighting is actually just straightforward, direct communication. This can be a shock to someone who isn't used to such directness from a partner who may have been less forthright during the relationship. Adjusting to this change in behavior, whether in a romantic or co-parenting context, can be challenging and is a common hurdle in the aftermath of a separation.

Mental Preparation

When entering into a four-way settlement conference, I always advise my clients to mentally prepare themselves in advance. A technique I recommend is what I like to call "car therapy." If you're coming straight from work, take a moment to sit in your car before entering the meeting. You could listen to an audiobook, enjoy some music, or simply sit and breathe in the quiet, with the air conditioning or the heater on. This simple act of taking a few minutes to breathe deeply can significantly increase oxygen flow to your brain, helping to calm and center you. This preparatory step is crucial because it ensures you're not overly stimulated before a session that could last upwards of two hours.

Many clients find it beneficial to engage in this car therapy after the meetings as well. It helps them clear their minds and settle their thoughts before transitioning back to work, home, or other responsibilities like school pickups. This process, while beneficial, can be mentally taxing, but less so than the alternative, which offers less control and can be more draining.

As the sessions progress, by the fourth or fifth meeting, it usually becomes second nature. You'll find that you need less time to prepare beforehand or decompress afterward. The initial discomfort fades, and the process becomes more routine, almost automatic. As a collaborative family law attorney, I also recognize the importance of decompression for legal professionals. While we may not always have the luxury of a lengthy break or a therapy session, taking short moments to mentally care for ourselves is crucial. We need to be in the best possible mental state to effectively assist our clients, especially in the early stages when more guidance and reassurance may be necessary.

I believe any attorney practicing collaborative family law would agree on the importance of these mental preparation and decompression practices, not just for our clients but also for ourselves. By taking care of our mental well-being, we are better equipped to facilitate these conferences and guide our clients through the process with greater efficacy and empathy.

When To End Collaboration

If participants decide not to continue with the collaborative process, it doesn't necessarily need to be a mutual decision. Even if only one person chooses to withdraw, the procedure to formally end the participation is clearly outlined in our initial collaborative pledge. This pledge specifies that termination of the process requires written notice to all involved parties.

Nowadays, this is typically handled through email, which is a shift from the past when we used to send formal letters. It's common to maintain a group email thread that includes both attorneys and the participants throughout the process.

If someone decides to end the process, they need to send a written email to this group. Once this step is taken, both collaborative attorneys are precluded from participating in any future litigation related to the case. This means that if the process is terminated, it's like starting over from scratch—essentially, you're back at square one. Any agreements, discussions, or concessions made during the collaborative process cannot be used in litigation.

Withdrawing from the collaborative process requires engaging new attorneys, incurring higher attorneys' fees, and resetting the entire case, which underscores the importance of commitment when entering into this kind of legal arrangement.

In Chapter 3, we've focused on the *skill* that makes peaceful resolution possible. Nonviolent communication is the bridge between "we want to resolve this" and actually being able to sit in a room and do it.

But here's the reality I see in practice: Not everyone is ready—or able—to do this on their own.

That's when you might add a third ingredient: a neutral guide. Not to take sides, not to give legal advice, and not to "fix" the relationship—but to structure the conversation, slow it down, and help both people move from conflict to workable decisions.

In Chapter 4, we shift from *how to communicate* to *who can help when communication breaks down*: Mediation—the most common crossroads between private negotiation and public litigation, and often the best next step when collaborative law isn't available or isn't a fit.

CHAPTER 4

The Mediation Process

When a person doesn't want to retain an attorney but still needs assistance in reaching a resolution, they may choose mediation over collaborative family law. If they don't want to hire a collaboratively trained attorney, I always suggest mediation as an option. At the time of writing this chapter, for instance, I have two cases that would have been perfect for the collaborative process. But for a variety of reasons, the other side hired attorneys who aren't trained in North Carolina civil collaborative law. In those situations, we can't use the collaborative model, so mediation becomes the best alternative.

I'm a North Carolina Dispute Resolution Commission certified family financial mediator, so if someone consults with me, I can't mediate for them directly. But I could represent them in mediation or recommend a mediator to them. Then, once they've reached an agreement, they can come back to me; I'll draft it up, and we'll make sure it complies with every applicable rule and statute under North Carolina law.

We can have court-ordered mediation or voluntary mediation, and I tend to lump them together when I talk about them. In child custody cases, mediation is required by state law; it's written in our general statutes. You have to go through child custody mediation through the court system, and it's completely free if you have a pending lawsuit. No cost at all.

So, if someone comes to me wanting to file a lawsuit for child custody, I'll help them do that. But I'll also say, "Attempt mediation first. That might be a good first step." If your resources are limited, that's especially important. Then, if it doesn't work out, hire me to litigate. We can even meet beforehand to prepare for mediation with coaching sessions.

In litigation cases involving property division (marital assets and liabilities), the court also orders family financial mediation. That's also required under North Carolina law. The difference is that, for family financial mediation, you hire certified mediators from the North Carolina Dispute Resolution Commission, or the court can appoint a mediator for your case.

I would never be an attorney and a mediator for the same client at the same time. For example, I recently had a couple come to me for a private mediation before either of them filed a lawsuit. They wanted to work out everything: child custody, child support, property division, spousal support—the big four. We worked through it all, I prepared a memorandum of their agreement, and then I told them to take it to an attorney who could draft a formal separation agreement.

Later, there were two things they hadn't discussed: spousal support and dividing a retirement account. So, they asked, "Can we come back and have another mediation to talk about those?" Absolutely. You can voluntarily participate in as many private mediation sessions without ever filing a lawsuit.

Another example: I had a child custody case where we were modifying an existing order. It wasn't a huge change—the child was in high school and wanted more time with both parents. Instead of jumping straight into litigation, we conducted a private mediation in my office. I represented my client, the father had his own attorney, and we brought in a mediator to go back and forth between the rooms. In half a day, we reached a settlement and avoided a long trial and court scheduling delays.

Becoming a certified mediator isn't easy. It's a forty-hour training course plus a test. There are very few North Carolina DRC-approved programs, and the training is intensive—role-plays, homework, the whole package. That's why I respect the process so much. Certified mediators go through a lot to earn that designation. We're invested in it, we believe in it, and we've seen that it works. While there are other certification programs out there, the North Carolina Dispute Resolution Commission's standards are high. That level of training and buy-in produces outstanding mediators who can help resolve almost any family law matter.

When I was already practicing collaboratively, I knew alternative dispute resolution fit with how I view family law. I focus on people's interests, not just the results, and I care about preserving family relationships. Becoming a certified mediator only made me a better collaborative attorney. Mediation has given me tools and perspectives I wouldn't have had otherwise. When I act as a neutral in mediation,

I see the process from another angle. That helps me in collaborative cases, too. My clients sometimes hear things differently coming from me because of that experience, and that can make all the difference.

Mediation in North Carolina

Mediation is another form of alternative dispute resolution. It's identified in the North Carolina General Statutes, and it's distinguishable from collaborative family law in a few ways.

I like to think of it like this: Collaborative family law can sometimes be a step up from mediation, and mediation can also be a part of collaborative family law. Oftentimes—and I don't usually use this phrase with collaborative law—but mediation can be that "last resort" before going to litigation. Or, if you need extra help from a neutral third party, you bring in a mediator. Most of the time, that mediator can help the parties get over that final hump, maybe it's just one or two last issues they can't quite work out on their own, and move them toward a resolution.

Mediation in North Carolina can take on different forms. You've got your court-ordered mediation, and then you have what I call private mediation. Private mediation happens before the court orders anyone to go to mediation. It's voluntary and can occur early in the process. People sometimes call it "early mediation." It's also a tool for unrepresented parties: folks who can't afford or haven't hired an attorney but still want a mediator's help to reach an agreement. That's still considered private mediation.

You can also use mediation within collaborative family law. And under that "private" umbrella, I'd also include what I think of as non-litigation mediation. For example, if a couple is legally separated and both have lawyers negotiating back and forth (outside of collaborative law), they can still choose to go to voluntary private mediation before anyone files a lawsuit.

Now, when we get to court-ordered mediation, that's when I describe it as the court "forcing" you. There's already a lawsuit pending, and the court can dictate when and how you go to mediation. In North Carolina, before you can appear before a judge in a child custody case, the parents must go through child custody mediation.

That process starts with mediation orientation. Orientation covers the custody litigation process in North Carolina and explains how mediation works. After orientation, you schedule your custody mediation with a designated custody mediator at the courthouse. Since COVID, it's not always in person; now you can do it by phone or via video call.

Courts rarely waive that child custody mediation requirement. The most common reasons are if there's an active domestic violence protective order or if a parent is incarcerated. In some cases, like severe substance abuse, where someone's in treatment, they might delay the mediation deadline so both parents can participate. Years ago, if someone lived more than ninety miles from the county where the case was filed, that was enough to waive mediation. But with virtual options now, that's not really a factor anymore, even though the statute still says mediation "may" be waived for that reason; it doesn't say "shall."

Another type of court-ordered mediation in North Carolina is family financial mediation. This kicks in whenever someone files a claim for equitable distribution—that's the legal term for dividing marital and divisible property. The court will order mediation within a certain timeline, usually within 90 to 120 days after the first scheduling conference.

> Family financial mediations often become "global" mediations, meaning they address more than property division. They can cover custody, child support, spousal support, alimony, and attorney's fees; basically, all the outstanding issues in the case. Most people prefer this approach because the other option is going to trial.

In court-ordered family financial mediation, mediators can be appointed by the court or chosen by the parties or their attorneys. They must be certified by the North Carolina Dispute Resolution Commission (DRC). The DRC certifies mediators and sets their standards of professional conduct—basically, the mediator's version of the rules of ethics. The DRC's certification covers mediators for Superior Court, matters before the Clerk of Superior Court, and family financial cases. In all three of those realms, court-ordered mediators are certified and held to the DRC's standards.

When Mediation is the Next Step

Often, when I consult with individuals—whether they are thinking about separating or are just recently separated—I start by listening. I want to hear where they are in terms of communicating with their separated spouse or co-parent. To me, that's a key factor in deciding when, and if, mediation is appropriate.

If people are still able to communicate, I often recommend collaborative family law first. It's an all-encompassing process, and in my experience, eight times out of ten it leads to a resolution. But when individuals can't communicate, when there's real conflict, or let's say one person has already received a letter from their spouse's attorney or their co-parent's attorney, that's when I shift gears. Before things get too far into the adversarial process and someone files a lawsuit, I'll suggest a mutual, voluntary exchange of information—financials, whatever's needed—and then we set a mediation date. We agree on a mediator who practices in that judicial district, and we get it on the calendar.

That tends to be the more common route in my area, especially because collaborative family law isn't used as much here. In Guilford County, and really across North Carolina, collaborative law is still a popular form of alternative dispute resolution. But many family law practitioners have different priorities. They start with the adversarial approach to push for what they want through position-based negotiations. When that happens, mediation often becomes the first real point of dispute resolution for the separated spouses or co-parents.

The Letter

Typically, when someone comes to me after receiving a letter from their separated spouse's or co-parent's attorney, it comes with demands. Sometimes it's the kind we're used to in collaborative family law, featuring clear, itemized requests, but often it's more adversarial in tone.

It might say something like, "I want X, Y, Z for my client. If you agree, respond within ten days, and I'll prepare the settlement documents. If I don't hear from you, I'll file a lawsuit." Other times, it's a cover letter that says, "I represent Person No.1. Enclosed is a Separation Agreement reflecting my client's position on issues A, B, and C. If you agree, please execute two originals and return them. If I don't hear from you in fifteen days, I'll file a lawsuit."

Those are the most common letters I see. And, frankly, the kind I sometimes send myself. But when I send them, I try to take the adversarial sting out of it. I'll state that my client has retained me to work toward a **global settlement** of the issues arising from the legal separation or to resolve disagreements over custody. I'll attach a schedule of requested documents, making it clear that I'm asking for a voluntary exchange of discovery: financials, paperwork, and anything else that's relevant. I also say that my client is preparing the same information on their end.

I'll ask for a response within two weeks, and if they need more time or have hired an attorney, I invite that attorney to contact me so we can agree on a mediator and set a mediation date, along with a mutual deadline for exchanging documents. If my client is interested in collaborative family law, I make that clear as well, noting that they've retained me for a global settlement through that process. I'll even suggest resources like the North Carolina Civil Collaborative Law Association so they can find an attorney trained in that method, if they don't already have one.

That approach often signals that we're not trying to be adversarial from the outset, but that we're advocating for my client's goals and requests. Still, not everyone sees it that way. Sometimes, especially if the other person is unrepresented, they read even that softer language as adversarial. In those cases, they might hire an attorney who immediately files a lawsuit.

I've had situations where lawsuits were filed immediately after my outreach. Navigating that with the client can be tricky, especially since I choose not to litigate certain matters outside of a very limited geographic area. With collaborative law and other non-litigation approaches, I can work with clients anywhere in the state. But once it moves to litigation in a far-off county in North Carolina, that's usually where my direct involvement ends.

The Benefit of Being Calm

Having a non-adversarial family law attorney makes a huge difference, mainly because of the perspective we bring to the dispute resolution process. And I'm saying "dispute resolution process" on purpose, because that can mean a lot of different things.

It can mean non-litigation, mediation, arbitration, or collaborative family law. When a person works with an attorney who isn't adversarial, they get someone who considers *all* those different forms of dispute resolution, not just the one-size-fits-all approach of "let's file a lawsuit" and push forward with that process no matter what.

Sometimes litigation really is the best option. But if you don't stop and evaluate the alternatives, how do you know it's the best? Non-adversarial family law attorneys throughout North Carolina take the time to think through every available path rather than defaulting to, "We're going to court, we're going to put this in the public record." And right now, with the entire state using electronic filing, everything is available online 24/7.

The second big benefit of having a collaborative attorney is awareness of the long-term impact on relationships. More often than not, court filings and sworn statements end up immediately straining relationships. Everything becomes part of the public record, which can affect individuals and their families for years to come, especially when older or adult children are involved.

The third reason is financial. Collaborative attorneys safeguard their clients' finances by weighing the costs of each possible approach. As we evaluate which dispute resolution option fits best, we also consider the bottom line. Attorneys who focus solely on litigation and who work strictly within that billable-hour model may not bring that same cost-conscious perspective.

That's not to say litigation is *never* the best choice. Sometimes it is. But more often than not, it's not. And when it's not, you want someone by your side who's willing to explore the other options first.

The Bulldog

When people are looking to hire an attorney, they are often looking for "the bulldog." They call and say, "I've heard the attorney my spouse hired is a bulldog—the best attorney in the county. Everyone's scared of them." And then they'll say, "I need someone who will go toe-to-toe with them in court."

That's fine, but part of my job is to explain what that actually looks like. And not just in terms of "I'm going to fight just to fight." I want them to see the whole picture. We need to review all options and discuss their family and financial situation to determine the best fit for their specific situation.

When someone is laser-focused on "the fight," they can't see beyond it. And sometimes that's when litigation might be the best option. But if that's truly the only thing they want, I may not be the best attorney for them.

In that first consultation, when I meet with them, learn their goals, and explain their legal rights and the interests they need to protect, if I determine that litigation really is their best path, I'll refer them to attorneys I trust completely. People I would hire myself if I had a litigation case pending.

But if I sense there's any opening—any willingness to consider other routes—we talk about those. And sometimes that doesn't even mean collaborative law, but what I like to call cooperative, a non-litigation negotiation. And often, that approach works.

That's the biggest message I try to share with those people who come in looking for "the bulldog." I tell them, "Let's talk about this." The biggest risk you take with your family, your finances, your life savings, and your retirement plan is handing it all over to a stranger and letting them decide what happens, and that's what litigation really means.

Non-Litigation Negotiation

Another option is non-litigation negotiation, which is exactly what it sounds like. No one is filing a lawsuit, but unlike collaborative law, there is no agreement not to file a lawsuit. So, the possibility of filing is always there. That can pop up at any time. Recently, I had two matters where we were working together, sharing information voluntarily, and then suddenly, lawsuits were filed.

In non-litigation negotiation, or what I call cooperative family law, sometimes one person has an attorney, or sometimes both do, but they've hired them only for advice and counsel, for drafting documents, or to communicate with their spouse or their spouse's attorney on their behalf.

What that process really amounts to is a voluntary exchange of information. We discuss our client's goals and hard nos to determine whether we can find common ground. Can we identify the things both sides are willing to agree on to resolve these issues? Sometimes that works. Sometimes it doesn't. And sometimes when it works, it just takes some time to get there.

When we're negotiating, it's often two attorneys going back and forth with offers, counteroffers, proposals, draft separation agreements, draft parenting agreements—sending revisions back and forth. Sometimes people redline the documents. Sometimes they don't. I even had a situation where an attorney didn't know how to redline at all and instead typed changes directly into a Word document in size 16, red, underlined, bolded font, every edit they wanted.

It can look a lot of different ways. But the biggest hurdle is whether the other side, whether that's the other attorney or an unrepresented party, is willing to come to the table in the first place. Often, they are. Sometimes, they are only willing for a short period of time. And if nothing's resolved in thirty days, they'll file a lawsuit.

That, to me, is a real hindrance. It can mean families get tied up in tens of thousands of dollars in litigation, sometimes even divorcing before they've resolved all the other issues. And once you're in litigation, you're stuck on the court's timeline instead of having that control in your own hands.

Control may not always guarantee a better outcome, but it can give you a say in when and how you see your children, or in how your finances are handled. That's almost always better than leaving it to a stranger. And that's what a trial judge is. In North Carolina, in your county, the public elects judges, regardless of their years of experience in criminal, civil, or family law, or even as a licensed attorney. There are district court judges across the state who practiced law for as little as two or three years before taking the bench. Whether they are on the bench comes down to winning an election or receiving a gubernatorial appointment.

When Negotiation Doesn't Happen

Strong hurt feelings are the biggest driver toward litigation—the need to fight, no matter what. Sometimes, even knowing that all of their private business, all of those hurt feelings, will be part of the public record doesn't stop people. Even knowing it may cost tens of thousands of dollars, leading to the possibility of zeroing out retirement plans to pay an attorney or taking so many days off work, they risk their job, people still want to fight. When strong hurt feelings take over, they can drive a person in that direction.

When I have a client, who is still open to different ways of resolving things, but their separated spouse is harboring strong hurt feelings that are so all-consuming that they choose litigation, that's when mediation becomes even more important. We can often negotiate an early mediation, even during voluntary discovery. And many times, I find the lawsuit itself is just a tactic by the other side to pressure a client into giving in on one or more points, so things start moving in their favor.

In those situations, mediation is one of the most productive tools we have. It allows the parties to hold on to that adversarial perspective if they need to, but still sit down with a neutral, trained, and certified mediator who has the skills to help them work toward a resolution. And often, when that neutral explains to both people what litigation will really look like, hearing it from an outside source, not just from their own attorney, can be eye-opening. It makes the reality of the process sink in.

> Hurt feelings can start to settle in mediation, especially with good mediators who are experienced as both attorneys and as mediators in alternative dispute resolution. By the end, there's sometimes at least some resolution, and sometimes there's a lot.

Global Settlement

Global settlement is the term I use to describe resolving all of the marital issues between two people. And when I say marital issues, I don't just mean divorce itself; it could also be between two co-parents dealing with things like legal and physical custody.

If we're looking at a full marital case, a global settlement means addressing everything at once.

- Equitable distribution and property division.
- **Spousal support** (which includes **post-separation support** and **alimony**).
- Children's issues like custody and child support.
- Other financial matters, including attorney's fees or long-term financial concerns, such as retirement plans.

And when I say retirement plans, I don't just mean the 401(k)s or IRAs people already have. I also mean the bigger picture of long-term retirement planning.

Discussing a global settlement in that first exchange is often a great way to put your intentions out there from the very beginning. With that initial contact, whether it's with the other party or the other attorney, I can usually get a really good picture, almost a forecast, of what to expect. That helps me set expectations with my client about the timeline. Even if it's just a rough estimate, it's useful in predicting things like: Will we be able to use collaborative law? Will we eventually end up in litigation? Will we be able to go to an early mediation, whether it's private or court-ordered?

That's why I find the initial contact so important. Being as open as possible in that first exchange and clearly stating that we want to resolve everything makes our intentions known. At the same time, it gives us an opening to see what kind of response we'll get. In my experience, that first response often gives me a strong sense of how the process is likely to unfold.

No Attorney Present

Sometimes, when people separate, their first step is to hire an attorney. Other times, their first step is more like, "I just need to get my bearings and figure out what to do next."

When people come to me, it's not always immediately clear what they're looking for. My paralegal usually does a little screening to figure that out. Do they want me to represent one of them in a separation? Or are they both looking for a mediator to help them through the process together?

I recall one situation where two individuals came to me wanting mediation. I don't keep notes from my mediations; it's all just from memory and reflection, but I remember how clear they were about one thing: child came first. Everything else—finances, property, logistics—came second, third, fourth, or fifth. Their main focus was to create consistency and stability for their child.

They managed to handle most of the other issues on their own for a while, but eventually realized that certain aspects, especially the financial side, weren't sustainable. That's when they needed more help.

In another situation, I was representing a client as their attorney in a court-ordered mediation. We started from a non-litigation, negotiation mindset. We sent a settlement offer, requested financial documents, and tried to keep things cooperative. But when we didn't get a real response, nothing open or transparent, I had to tell my client, "Okay, we've got to file a lawsuit."

At that point, I needed subpoena power. If the other side wasn't going to be open and honest about the financials, I had to be able to contact their employer and the banks to obtain those records directly.

And that's when we discovered what was really going on. The other party was siphoning off marital funds—literally whiting out a deposit on their pay stub and sending money to a separate account my client knew nothing about. We only found that out because of the subpoenas.

If we had stayed in the non-litigation lane, we would've had to just *trust* that we were getting the right information. And from the very beginning, my gut told me we weren't. So, in that case, litigation was the right move. We had tried the cooperative route, but when that didn't work, the court process gave us the tools to uncover the truth.

When Mediation Works

I think it's important to speak about mediation from two different perspectives: one as a mediator, and one as an attorney participating in mediation.

I recall one case in particular where two spouses reached out to me as a mediator. They both worked in very public-facing jobs and wanted to keep their personal issues private. Their coworkers, friends, and neighbors already knew they were legally separated because one of them had moved out. But beyond that, they wanted to protect their child and each other from any more unnecessary hurt.

They found me and my firm's website (www.lawofficeofmpp.com) through a Google search, and after considering the options available to them, they decided to mediate all of their marital and child-related issues. They hadn't quite hit the one-year separation mark required for divorce, still a few months away, so it was important to them to get everything resolved and be ready to file once they were eligible.

They were on the same page about divorcing, but they still had to work through issues such as property division, child support, spousal support, and even things like who kept the pets. I had them sign a mediation agreement that set out the ground rules regarding matters such as my fees, what I could and couldn't do as a mediator, and the basic standards of conduct for certified mediators. I reminded the parties of a few other rules.

- The mediation cannot be recorded.
- I can't draft your divorce paperwork. My role is limited to writing a memorandum of what you've agreed to, typically in a bullet-point list.

- I can't give legal advice or explain what the law means for your case, but I can direct you to where the law can be found.

Because I can't tell you how to apply the law, I keep family law statute books on hand for anyone who may ask to see them.

The parties understood all of that and were still willing to sit in the same room together. It was emotional. This was a decades-long relationship with a young child involved. One spouse came in with a bullet-point list of issues, and the other was open to discussing them. I started by asking, "What's your common goal?" It was heartwarming when they both said the same thing: establishing normalcy and consistency for their child. That became the foundation for everything else.

In just four hours, they resolved about 90 percent of the issues: child support, spousal support, and property division. One spouse had been working hours a week to support two households, which left little time with their child. Together, they agreed that wasn't sustainable, and that both parents deserved a close, loving relationship with their child.

There were a few things left on the table, such as retirement planning. But I told them they could always come back to mediation later if needed. In the end, they didn't. They had an attorney draft the final agreement, and contacted me to tell me that they'd resolved the rest of it on their own, and thanked me for assisting them in getting to that point without a second mediation session. I believe that happened because they were vulnerable in the mediation room. That shift in communication helped them carry the process over the finish line.

That's why I like keeping mediation sessions to about four to six hours. Longer than that, people get tired and start agreeing to things just to get out of there. Heavy emotions plus exhaustion are not a good mix. Half-day sessions, with the option to return, usually work best.

Now, wearing my attorney hat, I've also been in those marathon mediations that run until ten at night—twelve hours straight with no real breaks. Clients get exhausted, and people start caving just to end the session. Honestly, that's usually not healthy. But sometimes, in litigation, that's exactly how it plays out.

I had a case where mediation lasted that long, and although it was grueling, it ended up being strategic for my client. This was a long-term marriage. All the kids were over eighteen, so custody wasn't an issue. The outstanding claims involved property division, spousal support, and attorney's fees. From the start, we'd said we wanted a global settlement, meaning that rather than piecemealing each issue, we would have a conversation at the outset to ensure that the mediator and attorneys for the parties agree that we will work to resolve all of the marital legal issues.

But halfway through, the other side tried to walk that back.

At that point, we either had to schedule another mediation or keep going. My client was fine either way, but she didn't have the money or time to do multiple mediations. And with all the marital misconduct involved in her case, stretching it out probably wouldn't have helped her reach her goals anyway. So, we kept going. Twelve hours later, she walked away with a successful outcome.

> That's one contrast I've observed between acting as a mediator and as an attorney: the hours spent in mediation. As a mediator, shorter sessions are usually better for everyone. But as an attorney in litigation, sometimes the long haul is exactly what gets the job done.

Chapter 4 shows what mediation does best: it gives people a neutral structure when they're not ready for full collaborative representation or a knockdown, drag-out fight in court.

But mediation is just one tool in a bigger toolbox.

In Chapter 5, I lay out the full landscape of Alternative Dispute Resolution—the options, and how to choose what's best for you.

CHAPTER 5

Alternative Dispute Resolution

Alternative Dispute Resolution (ADR) is a way to classify all of the different options for resolving a family matter outside of traditional litigation. Of course, there's the court route of litigation, but ADR is typically non-litigation, and it comes in different forms. I don't do arbitration, but I do three of the other options:

- **Negotiations** (basic non-litigation negotiations)
- **Mediations**
- **Collaborative** family law

Depending on the situation, each of those three can make a huge difference in helping you avoid going into debt.

Early in my career, I worked on a case where the cost of litigation was just devastating. A set of grandparents had legal and physical custody of their multiple young grandchildren, and in just one calendar year, they paid over $66,000 in legal fees. And that was on top of raising multiple small children, all under the age of ten. Neither parent paid child support, so these grandparents were completely on their own—cashing out retirement, draining savings—doing whatever they had to do. They loved those children and would do it again in a heartbeat, but it was heartbreaking that it had gotten to that point. One of their retirement accounts was nearly depleted because of the legal process on top of everything else.

When the case came to the firm, both parents were parties to the custody action. The case originated from a divorce and remained ongoing for years after the divorce was finalized. We represented the one set of grandparents, while the other set of grandparents had already joined in the case. "Intervene" is a legal term meaning a relative, or sometimes even a non-relative, who has legal standing can come into an ongoing custody case to make a claim for visitation or custody.

There were allegations of abuse. The children were in intensive therapy. Both parents were in very turbulent relationships with new partners, and breaking up, getting back together, involving many others tangentially. It was complete chaos. And so, it made sense that relatives stepped in.

Once both sets of grandparents were allowed into the case, we had multiple hearings, sometimes lasting months, just to continue reviewing temporary schedules. Judges would try one arrangement, then revisit it when it didn't work. In North Carolina, parents have an extremely protected constitutional right to parent their children, even when there are substantiated allegations of abuse or criminal convictions. So even in this case, both parents were still granted supervised visitation. That demonstrates how strongly that right is protected here.

> At the end of the day, the standard is always what is in the best interest of the children. And in North Carolina, almost all family law cases are bench trials. That means it's up to a judge, who is a stranger to the family, to decide what is in the best interest of the children.

Our first review trial lasted about a month. Every day, all day, in court. There were numerous witnesses, therapists, and experts. During two lengthy trial reviews, both parents were found to have acted inconsistently with their parental constitutional rights. Custody was then granted jointly to both sets of grandparents, equally.

It was a sad outcome, but necessary. And then it became even more complicated. We had to go back to court because the other set of grandparents, who were supposed to supervise one of the parents with a child abuse conviction, weren't actually supervising. We had a private investigator (PI), one of the best in the area, who documented that the supervision wasn't happening. After more hearings, the judge gave our grandparents sole legal and primary physical custody. The other grandparents were left with a much smaller role, and both parents were limited to supervised visits, either with a licensed social worker or through a visitation center.

One of the grandparents had the ability to handle things without my help after everything we'd been through together. So, I gave them the tools—blank forms, instructions, spreadsheets to track payments and non-payments. I told them honestly, "You could keep paying me, but you know what you're doing now. You've done this long enough." They were so thankful, and I still keep in touch with them. Even now, if they need help, they'll call me, and I'll bill just for the time we spend. I no longer require them to leave a retainer because I know them, I trust them, and they trust me.

By my best estimate, over the entire course of the litigation, they likely spent close to $150,000. It's staggering. But for them, it was necessary. They loved those kids, and the children needed to be in a safe environment. So, in their late sixties, after raising children of their own, they started all over again with their grandkids. It was exhausting, heartbreaking, expensive—and also one of the clearest examples I've seen of why families sometimes have no choice but to step in.

This example is one of those situations where I would say, absolutely, you need to go through litigation. Alternative dispute resolution is not going to work.

This had started over one unsubstantiated allegation of abuse. But when I dug into many years of therapists' progress notes—for each child, all their records—I was just floored. I mean, I'm not a mental health professional, but everything I read, everything I saw. . . to me, it was abuse. There's just no way it wasn't. It was a gut punch. Honestly, it took me days to recover from going through those records, and I wasn't even the one living it. I was just the outsider reading it. So, when it comes to physical abuse of children, yes, litigation is absolutely necessary.

But I've seen the pictures. Whenever there's abuse of any kind, whether physical, sexual, emotional, or mental, it is incredibly difficult, if not impossible, to get those people to the table. First, in a safe way, and second, in a way that they can actually think outside themselves. Because custody is supposed to be about one thing: the best interests of the children.

And here's the other part: let's say, somehow, we did manage to come up with an agreement. All parties sign it, we submit it to the court, and the judge still has to sign off. Even then, the judge has the discretion to say "no." They'll go through the entire court file, see the history, and decide, "Nope, I'm not signing this."

Not Going Into Debt

Here in North Carolina, the perception that you will end up in debt and lose all your assets just because you're getting divorced is pretty common. We've got 100 different counties, which means 100 different local courthouses, each with its own way of doing things. For example, I live in the only county in the whole state that has two full-time, fully operating courthouses. There might be other counties with more than one, but they're not full-time like ours. And because of that, we're kind of siloed here. Other family law attorneys usually don't come into our county. So, the attorneys here know how to work "the courthouse game," so to speak—how to get hearings scheduled, and how to move things along. But even with that knowledge, it still takes a very long time.

Before the global pandemic, I would tell clients that it could take six to eight months just to get a child custody trial scheduled. Nowadays, if someone comes to me for advice (even though I don't take custody litigation cases anymore), I tell them it's more like twelve to eighteen months from the time you file a lawsuit to when you get in front of a judge.

The common belief is that litigation is long, expensive, and you're at the mercy of a stranger. And that's not totally wrong. In family law cases in North Carolina, everything goes in front of a judge to make a determination of property division (equitable distribution), **spousal support** (**post-separation support** and **alimony**), and children's issues (child custody and child support). A jury almost never gets involved.

Technically, there are only two types of cases in the family law realm that are completely tried in front of a jury—alienation of affection and criminal conversation, where you sue a third party, commonly the paramour—but it's very, very uncommon otherwise in family law issues. Otherwise, it's all judge-driven. And now, with the "one-family, one-judge" system being implemented in all 100 counties, you have to wait until your assigned judge comes back on the bench, whenever that might be, in the appropriate courtroom. It already takes a long time, and honestly, it's probably only going to take longer.

It All Adds Up

I recently had a client whom I helped with their initial separation, which involved property division, child custody, child support, and even claims for spousal support. Through mediation, we were able to work out most of those issues. But the kicker was that it only happened that way because of the court-ordered mediation during litigation. I believe that if we'd started with mediation right off the bat or even had two collaboratively trained attorneys sitting down with the parties, things could have gone so much differently.

Instead, by the time we got to mediation for all the financial issues—property division, spousal support, child support—we had already been in active litigation for about two and a half years! And it wasn't like we had an asset to value like a business or a house to be appraised. It was mostly accounts and debts, figuring out who would be responsible for what. And yes, maybe three months of that delay was COVID, when courts were doing the bare minimum virtually, but even if you take those three months out, it still took years just to get in front of a judge for the custody trial.

We had mediation in the winter of one year, and then the custody trial didn't happen for another few months. And even then, it had to be split into multiple days: April, May, then June, all spaced out five or six weeks apart based on the judge's schedule. So, think about how much that costs my client in attorney fees, even with me trying to be as efficient as possible—using associates and paralegals at lower rates and cutting unnecessary costs. The financial toll was real.

But honestly, the bigger cost wasn't just the money. It was the time. Their child went from elementary school to middle school during the course of that lawsuit. The child's needs changed completely in those years. And my client spent all that time seeing their kid only every other weekend because, until the trial ended, there was no clarity and no final custody schedule. By the time we finally got in front of the judge for the custody trial, the judge practically cut short my client's case and presentation of evidence on the record, saying right in the middle of the trial, "I'm a 50/50 judge. Unless you show me abuse, I'm going to order 50/50 equal custody."

And sure enough, that's what happened. The judge ordered joint **legal custody** and joint **physical custody** on a week-on, week-off schedule. My client ended up with the schedule they wanted, which was what we initially offered to the other side at the outset of the case, but only after two and a half years of litigation, expense, stress, and lost time with their child. That's the part they'll never get back.

> That's the real cost of litigation. Not just attorney fees, the invoices and bills you see on paper, but the emotional turmoil and the strain on co-parenting. The constant uncertainty around medical decisions, day-to-day parenting, and trying to meet a child's needs while they're growing up fast.

Four to six overnights a month for years, when your child wants more, is brutal. And when parents ask me, "What does litigation really look like?" this is the kind of example I share.

My duty is to inform every client of *all their options.* That's part of my ethical obligation. So, I always discuss litigation, but also non-litigation: voluntary mediation and collaborative law. Sometimes it's easy to rule out some options. Like if there's domestic violence, I'll still explain collaborative law, but my advice will be that it may not be the safest or most appropriate path. Some clients still choose it, even with a power imbalance in the relationship, and then we work to make it safe, meeting virtually or in neutral locations.

But what I see too often is attorneys who are very litigation-minded, traditional, stuck in the belief that court is the only way. I recall one client's case where the other side's attorney had that mindset, and it was cemented in their client's head. So, we had no choice but to litigate.

Now, North Carolina adopted the Uniform Civil Collaborative Law Act in late 2019, effective July 2020, with bipartisan support in the North Carolina General Assembly. So, we actually had the option to use collaborative law even after litigation started. Courts will place the lawsuit on hold, a practice known as a "stay," so the parties can pursue collaborative law efforts. But in this case, the other side didn't want that. Their attorney wasn't collaborative-trained and wasn't open to ADR. Therefore, we had to stay in litigation.

I've had other cases where a lawsuit was filed, and we still pivoted to mediation early, maybe six weeks after the filing of a lawsuit. Mediation was scheduled quickly, and the whole matter was resolved within three months with a global settlement. Those clients easily saved five figures in attorney fees. And here's the kicker—we still had to wait for the one-year separation period before divorce, but all the other marital legal issues were settled.

So, can you change someone's mind? Sometimes, yes. If the other party hasn't hired a litigation-minded attorney yet, I think there's a window. But across the state, I've seen it happen. More attorneys are open to ADR now than five or eight years ago.

And from the client's perspective, ADR just makes sense. Court is stressful and unpredictable. Parking decks, no cell phones or smart watches, waiting around not knowing when your case will be called, paying your attorney to sit there all day—all of that before you even get to the judge. And sometimes, after preparing for trial multiple times, the case just gets rolled because of scheduling. That's time, money, and stress most people would never choose if they really understood their options.

That's why, even when someone comes in panicked because they've been served with a lawsuit and have thirty days to respond, my first advice is: You've got options. Yes, we can file an extension. Yes, we can file counterclaims. But before all that, let's see if the other side will talk. Let's ask about collaborative law. If not, let's proceed with voluntary mediation now, before the court forces it six months later. Because at the end of the day, mediation is often less traumatizing, and it keeps the details of your life out of the permanent public record, which is huge when you have kids. Because one day, those kids will Google their parents' names. And no parent wants their child to read the ugliest parts of their divorce in a public court file.

Looking Out for the Client's Best Interest

It *is* possible to avoid going into debt when getting divorced, and here's a good example of how to make that happen.

A lot of times, clients don't stop to think about the fact that their eighteen phone calls to me in May 2025 are all billed at $325 an hour. They're not adding that up. What they're thinking is, *I have this question that needs to be answered. I have to send this email because I need to know what to do before I make this decision.*

And I get it. I'm the same way. I'm very cautious with decision-making when I know it carries legal consequences. I can only imagine how heavy it feels when those decisions involve your family, your child. *Am I making the right choice? Will this harm me legally?* Those questions are real. And that's why people pick up the phone or hit send on the email.

But that kind of thinking is very "right now." It usually comes from heightened stress, sometimes even paranoia, panic, or fear. Part of my job is to bring that back down to a manageable level. And in my experience, the best way to do that is through alternative forms of dispute resolution.

Another client I worked with came to me on the recommendation of another attorney. That attorney and I worked together on a local board, and she thought I could help.

At our very first meeting, I talked with that client about collaborative family law—the idea that *they* could come up with the solutions. Not the law or a stranger telling them what the outcome had to be, not a judge deciding for them, but the two of them working together. And they could do that because they were still able to communicate.

They'd been married for over ten years, a significant amount of time. They had separated once before, even had a separation agreement, then reconciled, only to separate again a few years later. This time, they both knew the marriage was over, and they needed to figure out a way forward.

They had two teenage kids, the oldest in high school, and neither of them wanted their personal business made public. Both were business owners who had built up a lot of assets, with minimal debt, and they wanted to protect what they had worked so hard for while making sure their kids were cared for.

From the beginning, my client told me there was no custody dispute. Once they each secured permanent housing, things fell into place. They agreed they didn't want their children living in an apartment; both wanted single-family homes. Once that piece of the puzzle was set, they worked through about 90 percent of their marital issues fairly quickly.

I think we had two collaborative sessions at first, then returned for one more when a triggering provision we'd flagged early on came up. That last session resolved the final 10 percent, and then we filed for divorce. Overall, it took approximately thirteen months from when they first came to me until the divorce was finalized. Part of that was just waiting for the court's process once we filed the lawsuit for absolute divorce. But in real terms, they had their agreements signed and about 90 percent resolved by springtime, and then we returned in the fall for that last session to finish things out.

What stood out in that case was that both parents had the same goals. They wanted to keep things private. They wanted to protect their businesses. They wanted their older kids shielded from the conflict. They were already in therapy, both individually and with their children, and they were able to look beyond themselves and beyond their marriage to focus on the bigger picture. To me, that's one of those ideal collaborative cases.

I'll be honest, I see that more often when kids are involved. When there aren't children, it sometimes takes longer. Without that shared focus, the emotional stress and hurt feelings can get in the way. People need more time between sessions to process it all and to separate the relationship from the business side of dissolving a marriage. And that's okay. Sometimes, instead of meeting every two weeks, we stretch it to three or four.

What I've noticed is that after that extra time—working with therapists, reflecting, talking with their inner circle—people often come back to the next meeting with a completely different perspective. One meeting might be heavy, emotional, and full of stress, and then the very next one is like night and day. Suddenly, we're moving through the issues: dividing assets, and deciding what really matters, like whether someone keeps the house but needs more time to refinance. Giving people that space often makes all the difference.

Chapter 5 is the big-picture chapter showing the entire menu: litigation when safety or accountability demands it, and ADR when the goal is to protect privacy, finances, and long-term relationships. It also makes one point painfully clear: the process you choose isn't just a legal strategy—it becomes the lived experience of your divorce. It dictates how long you wait, how much you spend, how much control you keep, and how much damage gets done along the way.

But once people finally see that landscape, the next question is which one to choose.

That's why Chapter 6 is where everything becomes practical. We move from *what these options are* to *how they actually start* and when it's time to call my law office and say, "I think I need help."

In other words, now that you understand the routes, it's time to choose your own adventure.

CHAPTER 6

Choose Your Own Adventure

Welcome to the beginning of the choose your own divorce adventure. Picture this: Someone calls into my office with a family law issue, and I'm there to guide them through the process. Let's take the example of a person who is looking to legally separate. They haven't taken that step yet, but they have children, along with assets and debts that need to be divided.

When that first call comes in, we gather some basic information. This isn't about digging deep into their situation right away; it's just enough to get their contact details and some information about their spouse. This initial data is crucial because we need it to run a conflicts check.

In North Carolina family law, this conflicts check is a vital first step. Our state licensing agency, which sets the rules for professional conduct, takes conflicts of interest very seriously. They hold that standard in high regard, and, as practitioners, we must adhere to it strictly. So, before we dive into the nitty-gritty of their case, we ensure there are no conflicts that could complicate things down the line.

This sets the stage for everything that follows. It's the first step in what can feel like a daunting journey, but with the right guidance, it can also be a path toward a fresh start.

Understanding the Conflicts Check

A conflicts check is essentially where we take a close look at the caller, who I like to call a potential client. We gather their name and, if we're thinking in an adversarial mindset, we also consider who the opposing party is. Now, I really prefer not to use the term "opposing party." Instead, I like to say your spouse, your separated spouse, or your co-parent. I believe this language helps set a tone that this isn't just a fight; we're working together to find a resolution that meets everyone's needs.

With that in mind, we look at our client list. This includes anyone an attorney at the firm has met with, anyone I've spoken to before, or even someone who called but didn't make an appointment. It's important to run that check on both names to ensure that I haven't met with their separated spouse or soon-to-be separated spouse or their co-parent. The law sees these relationships as having adverse interests. I can't represent, communicate with, or give legal advice to someone if they have an interest that's adverse to someone I've met with, or who has retained me, or who I've previously advised.

There are ways to navigate this, such as obtaining written informed consent. Some family law attorneys will meet with both spouses at the same time, but that's not how I operate. I prefer to focus on the individual seeking guidance. So, that's what the conflicts check is all about. We run it through our intake system to see if there are any issues.

Skipping the conflicts check could actually violate our rules of professional conduct. If I talk to someone who has an adverse interest in a potential client I've met with, or even a former client, it creates a problem. Although there are ways to move past that, the conflict check is typically one of the first steps, and it can be a bit of a challenge.

Often, the person calling hasn't yet separated and may not even know what they want in terms of advice. They might be hesitant to share too much information, fearing that their spouse will find out they're seeking legal advice or that any contact will be made. So, the first step is to reassure them that this is just an internal check and that no contact will extend beyond our conversation.

Sometimes, we encounter people who are so cautious that they don't even want to provide basic information. Unfortunately, this creates a barrier that makes it hard for us to move forward. There are stories, more like urban legends among family law attorneys, about individuals who will call every single family law attorney in their geographic area to conflict them out from representing their separated spouse or co-parent. That's where this cautious approach comes from; we want to ensure that no interests are compromised. It all stems from the nature of the law being an adversarial system.

Once we complete the conflicts check, we can proceed with more clarity and confidence, knowing that we're on solid ground to move forward with an initial consultation.

Gathering the Information

Our clients will receive an intake questionnaire with basic information. This step is really important, and I need them to fill it out or at least bring the information with them. We have systems in place that allow them to submit it online if they feel comfortable, or they can bring it along. If we're doing a virtual meeting, we can screen share, too.

The reason this is so crucial is that I don't want to spend the bulk of our initial consultation just gathering information. It's a major time-saver during the meeting. By reviewing their responses before the appointment, I can identify potential issues in advance and focus our discussion on what really matters. During our consultation, I'll highlight the issues I've identified, ask them how they ended up reaching out to me, and what brought them to this point. Then, I'll share what the law says about those issues and lay out all their options for resolving them.

Think of it this way: It's like going to a brand new doctor for the first time. When you get a physical with a new doctor, they always ask you to arrive thirty minutes early to fill out medical forms. Additionally, you need to bring a list of your medications, along with your family and personal medical history, any surgeries, hospitalizations, and so on. It's pretty similar here.

When you're coming for legal advice, you're looking for help with your current situation, your legal issue, and figuring out how we're going to resolve it. Just like it's the patient's choice regarding their treatment plan, it's ultimately the client's decision on how to move forward through the legal process.

All the Options

Once we get to the consultation, we often dive into the clients' stories. A lot of people want to share how they ended up in this situation, and it's really important for me to hear that. It's not just about jumping straight into the law and listing all the things I think need to happen. I want to understand their journey—how they got to the point where they need legal intervention.

Hearing their story helps me provide better advice. Sure, I'll explain what the law says, but after laying out all their options for resolving these legal issues or disputes, I like to take it a step further. Based on my experience, knowledge, and their unique situation, I can recommend what I believe is the best method for resolving their legal issues.

I spend extra time during consultations discussing this part because it's crucial for the potential client to not only understand the law and their legal rights but also to receive guidance on their best path forward. For example, if they have limited funds, prolonged litigation in the court system might not be the best route, but they must be advised of all of their legal options.

Or let's say you're dealing with a divorce, and you and your separated spouse can communicate, but aren't in a romantic relationship anymore. In that case, we can discuss whether you can tackle certain issues together or if you need an attorney to step in. Would it be better to have a mediator facilitate the conversation, or can the two of you, along with your attorneys, come to the table and work things out?

We need to consider what's important to everyone involved—what their needs and goals are, and how we can meet those within the limited time and resources we have. We're talking about things like custody and other issues that require careful division or sharing. We explore these different options, and if litigation seems like the first option, we'll discuss that as well.

Choice A: Litigation

Let's say there's been domestic violence in the past. And when I say domestic violence, I want to clarify that it doesn't always mean you have a protective order or something through the courts. It can involve emotional, physical, or mental abuse—basically, anything that falls under my broad definition of domestic violence.

If that's the situation, I'll share all the options, but when it comes to advising what's best for you, I'm likely going to suggest that collaborative law isn't the way to go if sitting in the same room doesn't feel safe. This applies even to a Zoom meeting; if being on a screen with the other person feels unsafe, then we won't do that. And if there's a protective order in place, we can't proceed with any direct contact.

In cases like this, we need to file a lawsuit, and I'll walk you through the steps of the litigation process. That doesn't mean we can't consider mediation, though. I often suggest private mediation, where you and your attorney meet with a family financial certified mediator, and you're not in the same room as the other person. This can be a great option, especially if cost is a concern or if assets are limited, like when one person has worked inside the home while the other has worked outside of the home.

As we explore different resolution options, we've touched on litigation, but let's delve a bit deeper into what that process looks like.

Once you decide where to file, you're bound by that judicial district's local rules. These rules are more specific than the general statutes or case law and dictate procedural details, like when you can file and how to get an emergency motion heard. They also outline when you're required to provide financial disclosures for what we collectively call family financial cases—property division, spousal support, and child support.

We have rules governing the financial disclosures we must submit and the financial affidavits we must complete before heading to mediation. In North Carolina, mediation is court-ordered for family financial matters, so before you can present your case in front of a judge, you have to go through mediation. The mediator's role is crucial in this situation. If you can't reach an agreement, they'll decide whether to recess and return to mediation or report to the court that you've reached an impasse.

In family law cases in North Carolina, most issues are decided by a judge, which we call a bench trial, rather than a jury. Ultimately, it's the judge who decides how assets are divided, how debts are paid, how much support is awarded, and how often you see your children.

That gives you an overview of the litigation option. We typically won't go into this much detail during a consultation unless we've really identified that litigation is the best route. If it is, we'll spend more time discussing it, because the court process is so nuanced, and we're at the mercy of the court's timeline. We have limited control over how quickly the case moves forward with litigation.

Now, let's talk about options that are less adversarial, moving from the most contentious to the least confrontational methods.

Choice B: Non-Litigation

On the adversarial scale, the next option would be non-litigation negotiation. This means I could either be involved as an attorney, or the two parties, such as spouses or co-parents, might negotiate among themselves. Alternatively, I could negotiate on my client's behalf to resolve all issues at hand.

There's still an adversarial nature to this method, and it tends to be very positional. We're talking about my client's position, and I'm going to negotiate with the other side to ensure I get my client what they want, no matter what. Honestly, I'm not overly concerned about the other party unless my client's goals are aligned with theirs.

Now, if my client's focus is on their children—like wanting what's best for them and ensuring they have X, Y, and Z—that becomes the position I negotiate from. So, even in this model, we're still in a position-based negotiation, which remains somewhat adversarial. There's no guarantee that it won't escalate to litigation, and that option is always on the table.

Often, people don't choose this route unless they're unsure how their spouse will respond or if they're looking to separate but haven't yet done so. They may have concerns about legally separating in North Carolina for whatever reason. Typically, I'll reach out to the opposing party, the separated spouse or soon-to-be-separated spouse, to see if they're interested in working towards a global settlement, resolving all the legal issues we've discussed.

This is usually the first step to gauge where they stand on the adversarial spectrum, if that makes sense. It helps us understand their willingness to engage in negotiations. Often, this initial step leads us to the next option lower on the adversarial scale: mediation.

Choice C: Private Mediation

I like to call this private mediation because it's not court-ordered. It's simply two people deciding they need to resolve their issues and want a neutral party to help them reach that resolution. When they choose mediation, we start communicating with the other side, whether that's the other attorney or just the other party, and ask for a voluntary exchange of documents. In legal terms, we refer to this as discovery, which is the exchange of information to help work toward a resolution.

We're still in that position-based negotiation model, but the mindset here is less adversarial because we're using a neutral mediator. No one is trying to get external intervention to resolve matters; the control remains in the hands of the parties involved, whether that's the spouses or the co-parents. This is why I'd say that on the adversarial scale, private mediation leans towards the least adversarial end of the spectrum.

With a mediator, there's a commitment to voluntary disclosure. Typically, we agree that two weeks before the mediation date, we'll voluntarily exchange documents, and that all documents are exchanged securely to protect everyone's information. The goal isn't to pull a "smoking gun" out of my back pocket during mediation or to get what I want at all costs.

In voluntary mediation, both parties have to buy into the process and come to the table with a willingness to resolve things without external intervention. I find this is one of the most common options discussed in consultations. People appreciate that they still have control and decision-making ability over their lives and their children's lives, rather than being told what's going to happen or what they can or cannot do.

They aren't just being handed a list of what they do or don't get. This sense of control is a big part of why people are drawn to this option.

Choice D: Collaborative Family Law

The final option on the adversarial scale is collaborative family law, and this is the focus of my practice. I find that it's one of the most beneficial processes within family law in North Carolina. Collaborative family law significantly shifts the mindset of everyone involved, including the attorneys and the parties themselves. It flips the approach from a positional-based negotiation model to an interest-based negotiation model.

When we make this mindset shift in the collaborative world, we call it a "paradigm shift." This change moves us from an adversarial to a non-adversarial perspective. It opens people up to thinking beyond their own internal bubbles, allowing them to consider the needs of the entire family. While some of this can happen in non-collaborative cases, collaborative law puts it at the forefront, rather than treating it as an afterthought that we'll address when we get in front of a judge.

In collaborative family law, we focus on the needs of both spouse A and spouse B. We have a finite number of assets and 365 days in a year—how do we allocate them between two parents? What will be best for the children? This process places those interests front and center, giving the individuals ownership over the decisions that will shape their future lives.

I often stress this option for clients when I see there's no history of domestic violence, according to my definition, and when they share their stories with me. If there's even minimal communication with their separated spouse or co-parent, I highlight how collaborative family law can benefit their family.

We determine the best course of action once the potential client decides which option they want to pursue. I can't make that decision for them. My role is to advise them. We have state ethics opinions from our licensing agency that require us to present all available options. Ultimately, the choice is with the clients—not the attorneys—and they choose the path going forward.

Choosing Your Non-Litigation Option

Once someone has made their decision on how they want to proceed, the first step in a non-litigation process is identifying and contacting the other party, whether that's the separated spouse or the soon-to-be-separated spouse. If they have an attorney, I'll reach out to that attorney first. I can't communicate directly with a represented party, but if I'm unsure about their legal representation, I'll ask my client if they know of any attorney involved.

If they do, I'll contact that attorney informally, maybe a quick call or an email, just to confirm their involvement. If it turns out there's no attorney, I'll reach out to the other party directly via email. I'll let them know that we'd like to enter the collaborative family law process, or work together toward a global resolution of all legal issues, and commit to voluntary mediation.

In that first email, I'll propose a timeline, suggesting we exchange documents by a specific date and aim to enter mediation within six to eight weeks. I'll also include recommendations for mediators in the local county where the parties live. It's essential to find a mediator who is certified, experienced, and local to that county, as they can offer valuable insights about what litigation is like in that judicial district.

I'll also provide a schedule of documents we need them to produce, and my client will do the same. This can include everything from bank statements and tax returns to pay stubs, business records, rental documents, real estate papers, mortgage statements, and credit card information—basically any financial documentation we might need.

At the same time, I always have my client start gathering these documents. This is where many of the subsequent steps occur: collecting the necessary paperwork and preparing financial affidavits. When I mention affidavits, I mean financial worksheets or **inventory worksheets** for property division, as well as budget worksheets (such as **cash flow worksheets**) if we're looking at cash flow analysis for spousal support and child support.

Once we've figured out which of the four big options we're going with, it becomes a lot of work on the attorney's side. I can't go to a bank and get these documents or subpoena them if there's no lawsuit. So, in a voluntary mediation or collaborative setting, everyone involved has to take responsibility for providing their financial disclosures to their attorneys. Then, the attorneys exchange those documents to prepare for mediation.

Preparation and Execution: Making It Happen

As soon as we have all the information for the mediation option, it's really up to the attorney to synthesize all the information so we can meet our clients' needs, goals, and positions. After we exchange the financial disclosures with the other party, we look to organize everything. Every attorney has their own style, and I'm old-school. I like binders. I love having things tabbed and color-coded. It helps me stay organized and prepared for mediation.

We have a series of meetings with clients to review documents, budget worksheets, and inventory worksheets, making sure there are no lingering questions. My perspective going into mediation is that I want all the information. I need to know everything, even if it's highly personal and sensitive. Sometimes, it takes time for clients to feel comfortable sharing private information with me. For example, if there's been adultery in the marriage, discussing that can be really difficult for both sides, whether they were the one who strayed or the one who was betrayed. It's sensitive stuff, and I want to give my clients the time and space to share that information because it's crucial before heading into mediation.

This preparation differs from a collaborative four-way settlement conference. Typically, in voluntary mediation, we have one main mediation session. We might have multiple sessions, but usually, it's just one that starts first thing in the morning and can run through lunch. I've even had mediations—both voluntary and court-ordered—that went until 10 p.m. People end up tired and drained, mentally, physically, and emotionally, and they might agree to things they shouldn't just to be done. I'm not a fan of those marathon mediations. I prefer a structured schedule, like 9:30 a.m. to 6 p.m. with a lunch break or to 5 p.m., working through lunch. If we need to take a break and return, we schedule that before we leave so everyone knows what to expect.

Before the next mediation, we exchange information with the other attorney to make sure nothing is missing. If there's something we need, like a bank statement or information from an employer, we keep a checklist of what's required before the next session. I think that's really helpful.

When it comes to collaborative four-way settlement conferences, the preparation is a bit different because we do the work during the session. We gather all necessary information beforehand. I review all the financials, and if I notice something's missing, I'll email the team to request it. For instance, if we're preparing for a session to discuss cash flow, I might need W-2s from the last four years and a year-to-date pay stub. If they just got paid the Friday before, I'll ask them to upload that information, as well as any recent retirement statements.

During a four-way conference, which usually lasts about two hours, we take a quick break—just a bathroom break—and then keep going. Before we end the session, we schedule the next one and come up with a list of homework for everyone involved. This way, everyone knows who is responsible for what before the next meeting, whether it's gathering documents, working on their budget, or drafting a proposal.

In collaborative settlement conferences, we typically don't have a neutral mediator at every session. Sometimes, a mediator can be brought in to help resolve outstanding issues or to prevent the process from escalating to litigation. But those are some of the big differences between collaborative four-way sessions and mediation.

Time To Choose Your Adventure

Now that you're familiar with your options, you have the power to decide how to proceed. Even if you're in the middle of litigation or a trial, at any point, you can say, "I'm going to make this settlement offer" with whatever information you have gathered. If the other side is willing to come to the table, you can negotiate, even during a trial.

Courts usually take breaks in the morning, one in the afternoon, and a long lunch break, so there's always an opportunity to present a settlement offer.

> This process is truly a choose-your-own-adventure, and it's never completely out of your hands.

Each person involved in this process has the ability to make decisions about how those decisions are made. Who's going to guide you in making these choices? Those decisions can come from a judge, both parties working through their attorneys, a mediator helping each side see different perspectives, or even from the individuals themselves sitting down together. It's about listening to each other's needs and goals and working collaboratively to come to a decision.

At any point in these four options, an individual involved in family law disputes can make those choices. If someone decides they want a judge to tell them they have to pay child support, regardless of what their attorney advises, that's their decision. You're choosing to have a judge make that call.

Now that you've come to the end of Chapter 6, you see that you're not stuck on a conveyor belt to court. You have options.

It's time to discuss the *first* decisions you have to make.

Because no matter which path you choose—litigation, mediation, collaborative, or something in between—real life doesn't pause while the adults sort it out. Bills still come due. Kids still need to be picked up, fed, and insured. Someone still has to decide what happens *this week*, not six months from now when the paperwork catches up.

The next chapter is about what you can't put on hold: What happens to your dependents while everything else is being worked out.

CHAPTER 7

What About the Children?

Some situations become truly collaborative, especially once all the legal issues start popping up. Let me give you a recent example.

This one began with a legal separation. There were kids. One spouse had acts of what we'd call marital misconduct under the law, and the supporting spouse, who worked outside the home, was left with some very deep hurt about their partner having a relationship outside the marriage.

But despite everything between them emotionally, they were able to set those heavy feelings aside when it came to the kids, especially anything tied to financial support and general well-being.

If you were to imagine a big jigsaw puzzle, some people build the puzzle by starting with the frame; this was like that. For those two parents, the shared focus on their children was the outer edge. It was their starting point and the one thing they came back to and agreed on.

Together, they were able to ask:

- Are we going to enroll them both in private school or send them to the local public school?
- If it's a public school, what kind, the local district school or charter?
- Can we both agree on this one?
- Can we afford a private school for all of the kids?
- Will they thrive there?
- Will their needs be met?

They wanted it to work, not just for the kids, but in a way that supported their shared custody schedule. It mattered to both of them that time with the kids wasn't one-sided. It wasn't "Mom-heavy" or "Dad-heavy." There are two homes now, and they both get it: it's important for the children to spend meaningful time in each one of them.

In that situation, the kids were the foundation, or border, of the puzzle. Having that common ground helped so much. It gave us a way to work through the trickier parts, like the financial pieces, because they were already aligned on how to parent, then to co-parent, in two homes instead of one.

This whole collaborative process pushes people to face their emotions and talk through things they probably wouldn't bring up otherwise. With these two parents in particular, the kid-related conversations were actually the easiest ones. They love their kids. That wasn't up for debate; neither of them doubted that about the other.

And that's what kept pulling them back into this collaborative mindset. It's what kept the communication nonviolent and constructive. Questions like: Where will the kids go to school? What kind of medical care are we establishing? Who will their pediatrician be?

Those questions became entry points. Once they started talking about their children, it opened up space to eventually talk about the harder, heavier emotions, too. It helped them figure out when to set those feelings aside and when it was safe to bring them to the table.

Your Dependents and What Happens to Them

The very first question that almost always comes up when people are going through a legal separation and heading for a divorce, and there are children, is: What happens with the kids? Everything else in the case might take months, sometimes even years, to sort out. But you can't just put the kids on hold. You can't press pause on them while the rest gets figured out.

That's why issues involving the children almost always come to the forefront first. And when I talk about "children's issues," I really mean two specific legal matters here in North Carolina: child custody and child support.

Here's something a lot of people don't realize: These are two completely separate legal claims. One doesn't automatically depend on the other. Just because you've got custody doesn't mean the other parent has to pay child support. And just because you're receiving child support doesn't mean you automatically have full custody.

There's a lot of nuance in how the two interact, but at the core of both is one key phrase we repeat over and over again: the best interests of the child. That's really the heart of custody law in North Carolina.

A lot of people come in asking, "Well, isn't this a mother's state? Don't moms usually get custody?" Or dads will ask, "Do I even have a chance?" That idea comes from something called the Tender Years Doctrine. Historically, the law presumed that during a child's early years, the so-called "tender years," usually under age seven, the mother, as the primary caretaker, should have custody. But that's not the law anymore. Today, the standard is what is in the best interest of the child.

Of course, that's easy to say. But what does it really mean? North Carolina courts have called the best interest of the child the "polar star" in deciding custody. And who decides that? The judge. The problem is that a judge is basically a stranger to your family. And when it comes to something as personal as your kids, your own flesh and blood, it's a tough pill to swallow to let a stranger decide what's best for them.

North Carolina law recognizes that. This is why, in the late 1980s, the legislature made child custody mediation a requirement in any custody case. Each judicial district has its own approach to handling this. In my district, not only is custody mediation required, but so is a parenting class. And no, this isn't about teaching people how to be parents. It's about shifting from parenting in one household to co-parenting across two. It's about learning how to navigate that transition.

Even outside of my district, even in collaborative cases, I often recommend parenting classes. Not because anyone's a bad parent, but because they help people refocus on what's really important—the kids. I've had clients come back from these classes saying, "Wow, I thought I was a great parent before, but I learned so much."

Once the class is complete, mediation happens. Usually it's at the courthouse, though sometimes we can bypass it. For example, if the parties wish to pursue collaborative family law rather than litigation, we can pause the court process and move the case to "inactive" status. That gives families breathing room to work things out outside the courtroom.

There are also situations where mediation can be waived altogether, like when the parents have already gone through private mediation, if there's a history of domestic violence, if one parent struggles with substance abuse, or if one parent is incarcerated. And if parents already have a custody agreement and just want it formalized, a judge can sign off on it without requiring mediation. I call that a "friendly lawsuit" for custody by consent of both parents. However it happens, everything still comes back to the child's best interests.

How do we figure out what that looks like? In collaborative cases, I often cite a North Carolina case that outlines five areas to consider: physical welfare, moral welfare, spiritual welfare, emotional welfare, and mental welfare. That's the lens we use to evaluate custody arrangements. Not what works best for the parents, but what truly supports the child.

When we talk about custody in North Carolina, it really breaks down into two parts. The first is physical custody, or the schedule of where the children go to sleep at night. For example: you've got Monday and Tuesday, I've got Wednesday and Thursday, we alternate weekends, or we go week-on/week-off. That's physical custody.

The second is legal custody, which is the big one. Legal custody is about decision-making. It gives a parent the right to make major life choices for their child, like medical, educational, and spiritual choices. That includes things like what school the child attends, which doctors see, whether they get certain medical treatments, and their religious upbringing. Since COVID, we've seen disputes come up more and more around vaccines, masking, and school safety. Those are all legal custody decisions.

Extracurricular activities sometimes overlap here, too, depending on the time and financial commitment involved. But legal custody is really about the big, life-shaping choices. For example, let's say you're trying to decide whether your child should have their wisdom teeth removed. It's not an emergency, but it's highly recommended and expensive. You have to ask: Will this help their physical welfare? Will it prevent pain later? That's a real-world example of where physical and legal custody meet.

> At the end of the day, every decision, every schedule, every plan should circle back to this one question: what is truly in the best interest of our child?

How Decisions are Made

Often, parents reach decisions through the collaborative law process. They sit down at the table, talk honestly about what's been working, what hasn't, and really hash things out. Collaborative attorneys will often help ground clients in that process by reminding them it's not just about what works for me or what works for you, but also what it feels like for the child moving back and forth between two homes.

Take schedules, for example. Sometimes that "2-2-3" split (Monday and Tuesday with one parent, Wednesday and Thursday with the other, then alternating weekends) just doesn't work. Having a child switch in the middle of a school week might not be the best thing.

Maybe carrying an overnight bag to school and stuffing it in a locker every few days is too much.

If the child is very young and not in school yet, a full week-on/week-off can be too long to be away from either parent. So, we look at age, routines, and circumstances. We ask whether the parents live close by. Even if they alternate during the week, can they realistically get the child to school on time? Or would the child end up sitting in a car for two hours every morning and every afternoon before and after school?

All of those factors matter. As collaborative attorneys, we try to help each parent see things through the other parent's eyes. Honestly, it is easier when both parents live in the same city. But that doesn't mean we can't work with other situations. I've seen parents make it work even when one lives in North Carolina and the other in Florida. Maybe they agree on every other weekend, and one parent makes the drive and stays with extended family. These solutions return decision-making to parents, rather than leaving it to a stranger in a black robe who only knows what has been presented in court. Judges base their decisions on the evidence, and in a temporary custody trial, they often have only an hour or two to get to know your family before making the call.

In collaborative law, we take more time. We look at what's been working, what hasn't, and whether the child has expressed any preferences. Parents often ask, "How old does the child have to be in North Carolina to talk to a judge?" The truth is, it depends. It's up to the judge. Some judges refuse to talk to children at all, whether in open court, an empty courtroom, or chambers. I've even seen a judge have a child testify in open court over the objections of both parents and their attorneys.

That's where collaborative law can really help. If both parents want their child to feel safe and heard, we can bring in a neutral third party. We call them child welfare specialists. They're usually mental health professionals trained in the collaborative process. They meet with the child as many times as needed until the child feels comfortable. It's not therapy. It's about building a relationship so the child feels safe talking. The specialist then prepares a report and provides recommendations based on what the child has expressed.

That kind of resource can make all the difference. Parents might hear from the child, through the specialist, "I'd rather do week-on, week-off. I don't want to switch in the middle of the week." So we say, let's try it. Maybe just for the summer, maybe for a couple of months, and then we reassess. Especially with older kids, it can help to experiment with different schedules and see what actually works best for them.

When Parents Can't Agree

Sometimes parents just can't put those strong, heavy feelings aside, and when that happens, we really don't have any other choice. By the time we get to that point, we've usually exhausted all the non-litigation options. That might be collaborative law, private mediation, or court-ordered mediation.

Now, private mediation feels very different from court mediation. In court mediation, you're sitting there without your attorney. In private mediation, your attorney is usually with you, and the whole atmosphere is different. So, when I say, "we've tried everything," I mean we've gone through those avenues, private mediation included, before ever going in front of a judge.

If parents still can't reach an agreement, we sometimes see judicial settlement conferences. That's where a judge steps in to help the parties reach a resolution. If the judge does that, they can't preside over the custody trial itself, but it's another option. It's not very common, but I have seen it work. Sometimes you just need someone completely outside the case to step in and help move things forward.

There's also arbitration. Personally, I don't like arbitration for custody cases, but technically it's an option. When all alternatives have been exhausted, the final stop is litigation. At that point, you're preparing for a custody trial, presenting your case to a judge, and letting that judge make the final decision about how the parenting schedule will look and how decisions are made for your children.

Sometimes, cases still settle on the morning of trial. Parents walk into court, see what's about to happen, and suddenly they're able to resolve things. Judges also often require a pre-trial conference in chambers. Basically, attorneys meet with the judge in a conference room and present a forecast of the evidence. Some judges will share their thoughts off the record about how they might rule. Others make their position clear right away: Unless there's abuse or some serious issue, they'll order 50/50 custody. Then, the only question is what that schedule looks like.

But if it doesn't resolve, you're looking at a trial. And a trial can mean days, sometimes many days, spent in court. It can mean grandparents intervening in the case to ask for visitation rights. It can mean the judge limits the time you have to present your case. It can mean lining up witnesses, teachers, therapists, and whoever you think is important.

And all of that is expensive. It's time-consuming. Parents have to take off work. Kids still need to be picked up and cared for while court goes until 5 p.m., and some judges will even keep going later if the time is needed.

> At the end of the day, when parents are so adversarial that they can't come to the table and work through what's best for their children, the control shifts completely. Once you're in trial, it's out of your hands and fully in the judge's.

Physical Custody Versus Legal Custody

Parents almost always still have visitation with their children, even if it's supervised. That might involve visits with a grandparent, another family member, a social worker, or at a custody visitation center. In those cases, they still have some form of **physical custody**, just through supervised visits.

Now, **legal custody** is different. The standard is just as high, but the way we describe it in the law is that a parent has acted "inconsistent with their constitutionally protected right" to parent. And for someone to act inconsistently with that right usually falls into three main categories: abuse, dependency, or neglect.

That's when child welfare law comes into play: when the **Department of Social Services (DSS)**, or Child Protective Services (CPS) in some places, steps in to make sure kids are safe. Losing legal custody is very hard to do, but if a situation falls into one of those "boxes" of abuse, dependency, or neglect, a parent can lose that right. And I say boxes with an open lid, because the law is always changing. Cases get appealed, reheard, or retried.

So, when we're talking about abuse, that can mean physical abuse. Neglect can mean abandonment, leaving children home alone, not feeding them, and not taking care of their basic needs. These are the kinds of situations where the environment gets so dire that a parent can lose both physical and legal custody of their child.

Child Support

Now let's talk about child support. In North Carolina, we have guidelines that give us a baseline. I call it a baseline because the guidelines really calculate the bare minimum of what it takes to financially support a child based on each co-parent's gross income.

Think of it like this: if rent is $2,000 a month and a mom and two kids live there, two-thirds of that cost is considered the children's portion, and one-third is the mom's portion. Same thing with utilities: what's the children's share? The guidelines take into consideration the bare minimum needed to support the kids.

North Carolina uses what is called an "income shares model." That means we look at both parents' gross monthly income, combine them, and then determine each parent's share. So, if Mom makes $5,000 a month and Dad makes $10,000, their combined income is $15,000. For two kids, the guidelines will give us a number, say, the bare minimum for two children at that income level. Then we break it down into Mom's one-third share and Dad's two-thirds share. That's how the basic child support obligation is calculated.

Now, custody doesn't control support, but it does matter which formula we use. The magic number is 123 overnights per year. If one parent has less than 123 overnights, then for child support purposes, that's considered sole custody. If each parent has more than 123 overnights, that's joint custody. And then there's split custody, which is less common, like when one child lives full-time with one parent, and the other child lives full-time with the other.

So, three different formulas, and a lot of fights come from which one applies. If one parent has sole custody under the 123 rule, only the other parent's income is used to determine the obligation. On top of that, we make adjustments for health insurance, for work-related childcare like daycare or after-school care, and sometimes a nanny. And then there's "extraordinary expenses."

Extraordinary expenses are rare unless the parents agree. For instance, travel can sometimes count if one parent lives in Florida and has to fly the child back and forth to North Carolina for visits. We average those flight costs into the support calculation. Private schools may also be included if educationally necessary or if both parents consent. Tutoring or specialized schooling may also count.

But there are things that are *not* considered extraordinary. Buying a car for a child, paying for their gas or insurance, doesn't count. I once had a judge tell me flat-out, "Your client didn't have to buy a car for the child." The judge said they could have bought an airplane, and it still wouldn't qualify as an extraordinary expense. Even though that car was being used equally by both parents to get the kids to and from school and each other's houses, the judge refused to include it. That's just the law. It's up to the judge's discretion.

So even with guidelines, formulas, and numbers, child support still raises a lot of questions. It starts with income and what counts as income: Are you self-employed? A W-2 employee? A 1099 contractor? Do you own a corporation? Some things the IRS allows as tax deductions, North Carolina law says, are still income for child support.

It gets complicated. Bonuses, one-time payments, retirement income, and disability income all raise questions. What if a parent receives veterans' disability or Social Security disability? Does the child also receive disability benefits through that parent? How does that factor in?

At the end of the day, it comes down to the judge. What does *this judge* consider income? What does *this judge* see as a legitimate extraordinary expense? What does *this judge* think is reasonable for one parent to pay for health insurance? It's all based on how the judge interprets the law and what they decide is the bare minimum needed for your child each month.

Child support is enforceable even if the original court order wasn't from North Carolina. That's because of a law called the Uniform Interstate Family Support Act (UIFSA). Every state has adopted it, and it allows each state's **Department of Health and Human Services (DHHS)** to establish and enforce child support.

If the original order came from North Carolina, DHHS can establish and enforce it. If it came from somewhere else, such as Arizona, North Carolina can still enforce it by registering that order here. Same with a Florida order. Once it's registered, North Carolina courts can enforce it if one of the parents lives in North Carolina. Each county has its own child support enforcement agency office, which is a branch of DSS, the Department of Social Services (DSS). They handle the enforcement of child support and even alimony in some cases.

The most common method of enforcement is wage garnishment, or what we call income withholding. Child support is deducted directly from a paycheck. In fact, in North Carolina, it's required by statute to be done that way whenever possible. That's usually the most reliable way to make sure support gets paid.

But what happens if someone loses their job? We saw a lot of this during COVID when people were furloughed, downsized, or out of work entirely. Enforcement became really tough. Judges were trying to balance everything. They were making sure kids had food, clothes, shoes without holes, jackets in the winter, while also giving parents a chance to be heard. Courts became overwhelmed and backlogged, and enforcing orders became even more difficult.

Here's how it works in North Carolina: child support is "vested" the day it's due. So, if the order says it's due on the first of every month, then that's the due date. If a parent pays on the eighth instead, it's still late, even though the payment was eventually made. Unlike some states, North Carolina doesn't charge interest on late child support. But that doesn't mean it disappears. Past-due support never goes away. I've had clients with six-figure arrears who even faced jail time for non-payment. And that's a catch-twenty-two. If a parent is sitting in jail, they can't work, and if they can't work, they can't pay. That doesn't help keep the lights on or food on the table.

During COVID, especially, a lot of parents ended up in jobs that paid less than their old ones. Their support had been set when they were earning more. Some judges recognized that and allowed temporary modifications, lowering support for a few months, then reviewing it again. That helped, but it wasn't a permanent fix.

Child support can be complicated. And yes, there are the absent parents who refuse to pay, but I've also seen plenty of parents who just fell on hard times. In my work as a court-appointed attorney, I tried to help those parents get job training, find work, or transition back after incarceration. Sometimes people just need resources, not punishment, to get back on track.

And that's when parents can't agree. But sometimes, parents *can* agree. They might sit at the table and say, "Okay, Bob, you're paying for the car our teenager drives back and forth, so let's factor that in." Or maybe one parent provides a gas card. A judge won't usually consider things like that, but parents can.

Same with extracurriculars. Judges don't have to consider expenses for travel to soccer, gymnastics, or even Olympic-level training. We've got case law in North Carolina that says even an amateur figure skater training at the Olympic trial level doesn't qualify as an extraordinary expense. So, the law doesn't recognize those things. But parents do.

That's the difference when you come together with a collaborative mindset and put yourself in the other parent's shoes. Judges are bound by what the law allows. Parents, on the other hand, have the power to consider the unique needs, talents, and realities of their own children.

Health Insurance

Health insurance for spouses is part of spousal support, while health insurance for kids falls under child support. And when I say spousal support, that's my blanket term. In North Carolina, we use post-separation support for what people think of as temporary alimony, and "alimony" refers to the ongoing support.

Post-separation support runs from the date of separation until the divorce is finalized. Alimony picks up after the divorce and continues, either as a lump sum or monthly payments, however it's ordered. And spousal support orders are not set in stone. They can be modified or terminated under certain circumstances, such as changes in financial circumstances, cohabitation, or remarriage.

And child support, of course, covers the children. Our child support guidelines in North Carolina include provisions about health insurance for kids: who provides it, what's reasonable, and how the burden gets shared. Those guidelines are reviewed and amended every four years.

In 2019, the health insurance section was revised to align with federal guidelines from the Department of Health and Human Services. Before that, orders would just say health insurance had to be "reasonably available." But what does that even mean? The revision spelled it out: "Reasonably available" means either an employer-provided plan or a private policy where the child-only premium costs no more than 5 percent of your gross monthly income.

That change gave everyone (parents, attorneys, judges) a clearer starting point. And even in collaborative cases, it helps. If both parents have employer-provided coverage, we can look at the options: Which one costs less? Which one has better benefits? What are the child's specific needs, and which plan best meets those needs?

That's the beauty of collaborative law. It gives parents the flexibility to shape the agreement around what works best for their family.

I believe collaborative family law is better for the kids because parents stay at the center. I'm pretty blunt when I tell clients, "You have control over how and when you see your kids." If you go through the court system, you're handing that control to a stranger in a black robe. A judge will tell you not just when you see your kids, but how you parent them. With collaborative law, you and the other parent create your own co-parenting plan.

Now, what works for one family may not work for another. A week-on, week-off schedule might be great for some, but not for everyone.

Others might decide to do what we call a "2-2-3," which is two days on, two days off, then three days on.

When I advise parents, I also consider the children's ages. For younger kids, say elementary school age and below, it's often hard to go more than two or three days without seeing a parent. That's why the 2-2-3 schedules can be a good fit. But if the kids aren't in school yet, sometimes a week-on, week-off arrangement works fine.

I even had one client do two-weeks-on, two-weeks-off until their kids started school. In that case, one parent lived in North Carolina and the other out of state, and it worked for them. But again, it doesn't work for everyone. That's the hard part, figuring out what's really best for your family during this period of transition.

Fur Babies

RUSTY M. PATEL

Another important topic that comes up during separation and divorce is pets. Pets can be as much a part of the family as children.

My dog, for instance, is part of my family. His name is Rusty. His adoption anniversary was about fourteen years ago, and his unofficial birthday is December 9, 2009. My family celebrates his adoption day on March 24. He's a pug-chihuahua mix, a "chug," if you will, with a little terrier in there too.

Rusty M. Patel

Rusty is my child. He's my soul. He even has a full name: Rusty M. Patel. In Indian culture, you take your father's first name as your middle name. Rusty doesn't have a father, so he took mine. That's how much he's part of my family.

But here's the hard part: In North Carolina, the law sees him as *chattel.* What's chattel? Chattel is property, like a sofa, a phone, or a laptop. The law treats Rusty the same as any other piece of personal property that can be given, sold, or otherwise disposed of. That's how pets are viewed in our courts.

Now, that doesn't mean judges don't care about animals. Many do. But they're bound by the law. In court, a judge can simply assign a pet to one spouse or the other, even put a zero-dollar value on them, and that's the end of it. I've seen it happen. And that reality is shocking when you think about how priceless pets are to the people who love them.

This is where collaborative family law makes such a difference. Outside of court, we can be creative. We can write agreements about pet visitation. We can decide whether both people will have the chance to say goodbye at the end of a pet's life, and what will happen to the remains. We can talk through practical things too. If one person is moving hours away, will there still be visits? Who covers vet bills, medications, dental cleanings, and prescriptions? What happens if a rental doesn't allow pets, but someone still wants to share time with them?

We can also include things like a right of first refusal: if one person can't care for the pet while traveling, the other gets the chance before the pet is boarded. These are the kinds of details courts don't touch, but collaborative law gives us the freedom to work them out.

And it matters. I've seen younger couples without kids but deeply attached to their pets. I've seen families where the children are as bonded to the pets as they are to either parent. For those families, pets are part of the restructuring process too.

Some judges actually support this approach. They want parents (and yes, pet parents too) to have control over their own lives rather than leaving it to the courts. Judges don't want to decide who keeps a dog or whether someone gets to say goodbye to their cat. They'd rather see families make those choices themselves.

> So, while North Carolina law may say pets are property, collaborative family law allows us to treat them like family. And that's exactly what they are.

Chapter 7 sits at the emotional core of this book. Some decisions carry enormous emotional weight for families in transition.

And sometimes those emotions are just too raw. As much as collaborative law, mediation, and negotiation are designed to keep families out of court, there are moments when those paths simply aren't enough.

That's where Chapter 8 begins.

Litigation is not the path most families want, and it's certainly not the path I default to. It is, however, a necessary part of the system. Understanding when litigation is unavoidable, what it actually looks like, and what it costs—financially, emotionally, and relationally—is critical.

CHAPTER 8

Litigation

My caseload is only about 15 percent litigation cases, and even then, the percentage that actually make it to trial is very small. If you look at civil cases overall, the averages are like 5 percent that go to trial, and the other 95 percent settle before getting that far. I'd say that's pretty accurate for me, too, and I like my caseload the way it is.

Most of my cases that have actually gone to trial were during COVID and right after. People just could not work anything out with the added stress of the pandemic. I probably had three cases during COVID that dragged on forever, like nine to twelve months, just to get to trial.

During a custody litigation case many years ago, I represented a client who had a history of drug addiction. She had gone to inpatient and outpatient rehab several times and experienced multiple relapses, but by the time she came to me, she had been sober for almost three years. However, her co-parent had taken out cyberstalking, assault-type charges just to prevent her from having access to their shared child, so she had no visitation rights whatsoever.

Our goal was to get a judge to make a ruling that would allow her to see her child. Because we were in litigation, and the custody case fell into the depths of the court system, the process took two and a half years.

For this case alone, I prepared for trial three different times. During a pretrial conference with the judge in his chambers (a time that allows a judge to forecast our evidence, meaning give the attorneys an idea of how he'll rule), he told me "I wouldn't want my kid to date this person, but there's nothing you've told me that will prevent her from being a good parent given the time and opportunity."

My client had taken the initiative to become a better parent by signing up for voluntary parenting, child CPR, and other classes to learn how to keep her child safe. She had also continued getting support for her mental health and working hard to maintain her sobriety.

I believe the case should not have had to drag on as long as it did. It didn't have to be as expensive or emotionally draining as it ended up being. Had Mom and Dad been able to sit down together and come up with a plan, or at the very least, had the parties allowed their attorneys to confer in non-litigation negotiation, the process could have taken much less time.

I'm pleased to share that with the assistance of her parents, Mom began to repair her relationship with her child, who was only a toddler when she'd lost visitation. At first, Mom was allowed supervised visits and eventually, through the litigation process, we graduated the schedule to increase their contact and time together. And now each parent has the custodial time they desire with their child.

When Family Law Disputes Lead to Litigation

There are situations in which the parties absolutely must go to litigation. No question.

Anytime I see allegations of domestic violence (whether it's a 50B filing, a temporary or permanent protective order, or even pending criminal charges like assault on a female or strangulation), I take that very seriously. Whenever those issues are present, I know collaborative law is not the right path because collaborative family law is about vulnerability, sitting together (in person or virtually) to talk about feelings and needs.

When that's the case, I'll tell my client, let's see if the other side will get an attorney, and maybe I can negotiate directly. But if not, then we need to file a lawsuit.

Whenever there's abuse (physical, emotional, mental, or sexual), it's almost impossible to get those people to the table. One, you can't do it safely. And two, they can't think outside of themselves. With custody, it always comes back to the best interests of the children.

Even if we somehow reach an agreement and everyone signs it, the judge still doesn't have to sign off on it. Judges review the whole court file, and if something doesn't sit right, they'll just say, "I'm not signing this."

Another telltale sign that a family law dispute is headed toward litigation is when a client says there's been financial misconduct.

The problem is that it's often really hard to get the proof. With finances, there's always a paper trail, but finding it and getting it into court can be another story. Sometimes I can use my economics background to do a kind of forensic analysis myself, and sometimes I have to bring in a third-party contractor. If I do that, I hire them so the work product isn't discoverable in litigation. Either way, it takes time and digging. And usually, that's when it's clear we need to litigate.

I told a story about a case where the wife was altering her pay stubs. She would electronically alter the numbers and type in new amounts to cover up money that was being siphoned into hidden accounts. She was wiping out balances, moving funds around, and making it all look legitimate. We call that the diversion and concealment of marital funds. In North Carolina, that's considered marital misconduct. But it's also the kind of thing that's really hard to prove without litigation.

Why? I touched on this in an earlier chapter, but with litigation, I have subpoena power. I can issue subpoenas to banks and financial institutions. And when those places tell you they can only go back two or seven years? Not true. With a subpoena, I've gone back over twenty years. It just takes time and can be costly.

Now, it's not always simple. If a financial institution doesn't have a registered agent in North Carolina, it gets cumbersome. Take USAA, for example. Many years ago, I had to domesticate a subpoena in Texas, then have it served under Texas law. I even had to bring in a Texas attorney to handle service. So, it gets expensive. But there are ways. And with the power of the court, the ability to order documents and enforce disclosure, sometimes that's the only way to get to the truth when someone's been hiding money.

Because there's always a money trail. That's why, in these cases, I say, "Let's go to litigation." Without subpoena power—without court orders—it's almost impossible to get full disclosure. And full disclosure is the key to collaborative law. Everything has to be on the table. Nothing hidden in your back pocket, waiting to pop out at the most inopportune moment.

> Now, with litigation, people can and will often play games. They can stall. They can refuse to provide anything, even when ordered by a Judge. And sometimes that means months of drawn-out court battles. But if the other side isn't going to open up willingly, litigation is the only real option.

I had a case recently where I wanted it to be collaborative, but the other side didn't even hire a collaborative attorney and actually refused to do so because their spouse hired me. We'd been trying to negotiate outside of court, but there was clear financial misconduct and a refusal to turn over financial documents.

And here's the kicker: There were adult children involved. Those kids gave loans to the other party, and my client had no idea. Once my client found out, they just wanted it over quickly. But I kept asking my client, are you really willing to cut off your nose to spite your face? Do you want it over fast, even if it means not getting the full picture?

This was a forty-year-plus marriage—decades of financial misconduct. There were also no minor kids to protect. In a situation like that, litigation is almost always the best option.

When Lawsuits Get Dropped

Whether you're in court-ordered mediation or private mediation, once a divorce case moves into litigation, there's usually an early mediation step.

Here's what that means. Often, when people finally reach a resolution, the settlement documents include a section stating that the plaintiff, person X, will dismiss their lawsuit. It can be a voluntary dismissal, with or without prejudice, depending on whether the agreement resolves all issues. That dismissal effectively ends further litigation.

Now, sometimes one party still wants a court order that says, "X, Y, and Z." And we can do that. Those are called consent orders, basically agreements that a judge signs off on.

Here's the thing, though: a judge doesn't have to sign it. That's the risk with consent orders. But more often than not, judges will approve them.

So even in mediation, we have options. We can frame the agreement and resolve the marital issues in a way that works best for our clients, for the parties involved, and, honestly, for their family as a whole.

Although families rarely hope to end up in litigation, many arrive there after exhausting other paths—collaboration, negotiation, mediation—only to find that resolution still feels out of reach. When that happens, the legal process becomes the structure that helps move families forward.

But guiding people through conflict toward resolution is only part of the story. The path to serving families and communities is often shaped long before an attorney steps into a courtroom.

In Chapter 9, I will take you through my service-centered journey.

CHAPTER 9

That I May Serve

Helping clients transition to the next season of their lives: That's really what the practice of law is. You're serving people—making sure their needs are met. And for me, service has always come naturally.

As I've already mentioned, my alma mater, Virginia Tech, has a motto in Latin, which translates to: *That I May Serve.* And that has stuck with me ever since I first heard it. Service isn't just a word on a banner; it's the cornerstone of being a Hokie. It's a way of life I've carried with me since graduating in 2008.

Law school was less about service and more about survival, just getting through. But once I became a licensed attorney (after a long struggle with the bar exam), I knew I wanted my work to be about more than just cases. I wanted to make the profession itself better.

That has meant being an example for other women, especially South Asian and Indian women who want to be lawyers but don't always see themselves represented.

> My driving force is to make sure women's names are spoken in rooms where decisions are made, as well as to ensure the safety of women who are marginalized under the law.

I take pride in my involvement with local, state-wide, and national bar associations, including:

- Becoming the first two-time president for the North Carolina Association of Women Attorneys, since the organization's founding in 1978
- Chairing the Women in the Profession Committee for the largest voluntary bar in North Carolina
- Joining the Board of Directors for the National Conference of Women's Bar Associations as an affiliate of the American Bar Association

As I write this, I have just become the past president of the Greensboro Bar Association, where I was one of the youngest presidents and the first South Asian.

The point has always been the same: If someone says my name in a room, then it's my turn to say the names of other women.

What's been most meaningful has been hearing from law students, especially Indian women, who tell me, "I'm so glad to see someone who looks like me in this role." I never had that. I didn't see anyone who looked like me leading bar associations or serving on the North Carolina State Bar Council, where I now sit as one of sixty-six members, the only South Asian, and one of the youngest councilors.

And that's really what it comes back to: service. Service to clients, the community, and the profession. Service that lifts others up and makes sure their names are spoken.

When I spoke at the Virginia Tech commencement ceremony, I felt compelled to share three big takeaways for the students. I will share them with you, too, because I believe they can help as you embark on your divorce journey.

Big Life Takeaway: Education

I deeply value education because that's something no one can ever take away from you. As I told the graduates in my commencement speech at Virginia Tech, "Your education is one of your greatest possessions that no one can take away from you."

A lot of people never imagine they'll end up in a place where they're going through a legal separation or a divorce. But once you find yourself there, one of the most valuable things you can do is educate yourself about your rights. What am I entitled to under the law? How can I protect myself now and in the future? How do I pursue the outcomes I want and actually achieve them?

It's so important to understand the law in your jurisdiction and how it applies to you—your life, your relationships, your future. What do you want to preserve? What do you want your next chapter to look like? The only way to make those decisions with clarity is to learn your options.

And it's not just about court. Education also means understanding alternative dispute resolution and the different ADR methods that can help you not only reach your goals but also protect your rights. That knowledge gives you something powerful in a season when it feels like everything is out of your control. It gives you a voice at one of the most stressful, emotional times in your life.

So, what does education look like when you're in North Carolina, separated from your spouse, or suddenly in conflict with your co-parent? It looks like learning the law. Learning your options. Knowing the situation is not forever.

This is a transitional period, one that's unsettling, sometimes painful, and definitely not easy. That's just the reality. But knowing your options helps ease that discomfort. It helps you find the path that's best for you and your family.

Because let's be real: The transition changes everything. Your lifestyle. Your finances. Maybe your career. How and when you see your children. How you live your life day to day. Sitting in that discomfort is hard, but it becomes more bearable when you understand your rights and know your choices.

For some people, collaborative family law might be the right fit. For others, a different approach may be the best fit. But the only way to know which is best is to talk to an attorney, get a real education about the laws that apply to your specific situation, and figure out your best option. There's no cookie-cutter answer. You won't find it by Googling or asking ChatGPT(or other AI tools). Every family and every life circumstance is unique.

That's why the first step is always: learn the law. Learn what it means for you. From there, you can make informed decisions for yourself and your family.

And even though it doesn't feel like it right now, this process *will* change your life. It'll change how you operate, how your family is structured, how you function in the long run, and how you communicate with your family. These relationships don't just end. They continue in new forms, and they ripple out into every area of your life, from your career to where you live to how you live.

My hope is that, through education, this transition will move you into a better situation than the one you're sitting in now.

Big Life Takeaway:
Grit

I want you to be gritty as you move forward in this transitional period and as you come out of it into a new season of your life. To get there, we all go through significant distractions and challenges.

To have grit is to have that perseverance—the ability to keep going so you can reach the long-term vision you have for your life. It's about pushing through the obstacles, the setbacks, the moments you never thought you'd have to face, like a legal separation or a custody battle, and still finding a way to put one foot in front of the other.

For me, grit looked like continuing to live for my fallen classmates and professors after the devastating tragedy in 2007 at Virginia Tech, when a student went on a shooting spree and killed thirty-two people and wounded many others.[1] For you, grit might mean moving forward for your family, staying steady through separation, and pushing toward peace and stability on the other side.

And grit isn't just about you. It's about your whole family. Having the grit to push through the muddy waters of separation or conflict with a co-parent to reach peace. In divorce, custody disputes, or separation, the goal is usually the same: reaching peace.

But let me be clear: Peace isn't some "light at the end of the tunnel." Peace is a calm you carry with you as you move into the next phase of your life. Because the tunnel doesn't end with divorce. Life continues. And what you really want is not just to get through this one year, or this year-and-a-half period. It's to build a happy, prosperous, stable family and life for the long term.

Angela Duckworth, a psychologist and Professor at University of Pennsylvania who researches grit, says, "It's staying loyal to what you said you were going to do, even when it would be easier to give up." And that's exactly what grit looks like in this season. It would be so much easier to lie down, to give up, to stop thinking about your long-term future. But we're not going to do that.

We're going to get up. We're going to keep going. We're going to work together to figure out how you can achieve your long-term goals, and how I can help you do that, whether it's through collaborative family law, mediation, or, if necessary, litigation.

---

1 Virginia Tech Special Collections and University Archives, "April 16, 2007: Virginia Tech Shooting," Virginia Tech Libraries, https://guides.lib.vt.edu/specialcollections/vt/april16

But either way, we're not giving up. We're going to keep moving through those muddied waters until you get to the life you've envisioned, the one where your family looks and feels the way you want it to.

Big Life Takeaway: A Strong Foundation

I talked about grit, about how you get through the tough times and find that peace on the other side of the tunnel. Not the light at the end, but peace as you continue living your life.

That might sound easy for me to say now, but the truth is everyone has their own path, their own obstacles and distractions. And for me, my foundation, the thing that got me through, comes from my family.

My parents emigrated from India in the mid 1970s. They were the first in both their families to leave and start a new life in a foreign country. They knew that no matter what, education would be the thing that changed our lives forever. That was their focus—their promise.

From the outside, our family's story might look like the "American dream." I'm the youngest of three. My sister is a clinical pharmacist at a large teaching hospital, my brother is a surgeon in Detroit, and I'm a lawyer with my own firm. But let me tell you, it did not come easy. It took grit, perseverance, and leaning hard on that foundation to get through the muddied waters, especially when it felt like there was nothing on the other side.

For me, one of those times was law school and the bar exam. I started law school in the fall of 2008, just three months after graduating from college. That transition was tough enough on its own, and then came the real challenge: passing the North Carolina licensure exams. Licensure is the official government process that grants an individual permission to practice a regulated profession. It requires meeting minimum competency, ethical, and character standards.

After graduation, I threw myself into studying for the bar. Twelve weeks of intense prep. I followed the plan, did all the work, and cut out distractions. And then the results came back. I missed passing by two points. Two points.

It was crushing. Watching friends and classmates celebrate, seeing their "congratulations" letters, while mine said otherwise, was one of the hardest moments of my life. I felt ashamed. Embarrassed. I kept asking myself: *Why didn't I pass? I did everything right. Am I not cut out for this?*

My mom was the one who picked me back up. She reminded me that it wasn't the end. So, I regrouped, studied again, followed the plan even more diligently, and sat for the bar a second time. This time, I felt confident. Assured. I believed I would pass.

But I didn't. I missed by four points.

That second failure was devastating. I'd gotten through three years of law school, and yet this was the wall I couldn't seem to climb. I felt stuck in the tunnel with no way out, swallowed up by embarrassment and doubt.

But eventually, I found my footing again. A few weeks later, I signed up for a third try. I met with a former employer, talked with my family, and my tribe. They all said the same thing: "Keep going." I questioned, *Do I do it differently this time?* So, I worked with a tutor, adjusted my strategy, and, strangely enough, studied less but smarter.

That summer, I walked into the livestock barn at the North Carolina State Fairgrounds, the place where the exam was being held. And of course, the obstacles came. A thunderstorm rolled in, the power went out, and there we all were, hundreds of us, in the dark, sweating in July heat and humidity, trying to take the bar exam. My laptop battery just barely lasted through it.

The second day wasn't much better, chainsaws, wood chippers, all kinds of noise from the fairgrounds. Definitely not ideal testing conditions. But somehow, I made it through.

A month later, a small envelope arrived in the mail. My stomach dropped because I thought, *This looks just like the other two*. I opened it, bracing myself. But this time was different.

This time, I passed.

Relief doesn't even begin to cover my feelings. After a year of fighting through failure and self-doubt, I finally had the letter I'd dreamed of since I was a teenager. I could finally call myself a lawyer.

I share this because life will throw you challenges. Big ones. Ones that feel impossible to get through. And in those moments, you may think there's no way out of the tunnel. But there is. It takes grit, it takes foundation, and it takes time.

And I'm here to tell you: You can push through. You can find peace on the other side.

Becoming a Lawyer

When I was fourteen, my vocation became clear. At my school, the dreaded Forum project was like a rite of passage before high school. Every eighth grader had to do it: research a controversial topic, write an eight-page positional paper, and then give a speech. After your speech, you faced someone on the counter-position, answered questions from a panel, and then from the audience. And the audience wasn't just made up of classmates. It could be teachers, parents, or even community members. Basically, the whole town could show up. At the time, it kind of felt like community hazing before moving on to high school.

The topic I wanted was about whether children who commit crimes like murder should be tried as adults, but it was assigned to someone else. Instead, I was given "The constitutionality of the death penalty in the United States." I wasn't thrilled, but I went with it.

Looking back, I was lucky. My sister was in college at the University of Virginia, so I got to visit her and use a real college library for my research. To fourteen-year-old me, that was the most exciting part of my research. I loved to read, and suddenly I was in this massive library with endless resources. (There was no high-speed internet at home back then.) I was in heaven.

I dug in. I researched the origins of the death penalty in the U.S., when it was ruled constitutional or unconstitutional, and why. I looked at the different methods states used and how each one approached it. I had to build an argument for why it was constitutional, even though, personally, at the time, I believed it wasn't. That was the assignment, so I had to figure out how to make that case and persuade the panel.

That meant sifting through all the research, deciding what was relevant, and preparing for the tough questions. Why did I think it was constitutional? Could I defend that position? On top of all that, I had to give a speech, and at fourteen, public speaking was definitely not my strength. (Now I can talk to a wall for fourteen hours straight, but back then, not so much.)

That whole experience—the research, the writing, the speech, the debate—changed everything for me. It cemented in my mind that I needed to be a lawyer. I wanted to help people. I wanted to protect people's rights. That spring of 2000 was a pivotal moment in my life. From then on, I knew everything I learned and everything I did had to point toward becoming a lawyer.

I didn't know exactly how I'd help people yet. But I knew this was the path.

Upbringing and Experiences

My family is my foundation—the source of my roots, and my values. My parents came to this country with almost nothing. My dad was already a medical doctor in India, but when he arrived here, he had less than ten U.S. dollars in his pocket and worked as a security guard at a Panasonic building. From there, he managed to pass his board exams, was accepted into a residency program, went through residency, completed a fellowship, and finally finished all the training required to practice as a medical doctor in the United States. Out of that, he built a home and a life for our family.

The challenges and obstacles my parents faced in the 1970s didn't end when they got through them. They understood how lucky they were to be able to create this life through hard work, and with that came responsibility: to give back. Gratitude had to be shown, and it wasn't just words. It was service. That value of giving back was instilled in my siblings and me from a young age.

For us, that started with volunteering. My mom always took us to the Danville Public Library. We practically lived there every summer. The librarians knew us well. We were there almost every day, reading books, using the resources, and hanging out in the stacks of literary choices. My brother loved computers, my sister and I would curl up with books. I parked myself in front of *The Babysitters Club* series for at least three summers straight.

Since we got so much out of that library, my mom taught us it was our responsibility to give back. So, we volunteered. My sister greeted everyone who visited the library and helped anyone find the books they were looking for. I reshelved books and helped with the younger kids who visited, and my brother helped with the computers and the emerging technology that the public library implemented. We each found ways to contribute so that other people in our community could enjoy the library the way we did.

Another place that shaped me was the YMCA. Danville is a small community, and the YMCA was where we took swimming lessons and learned life skills. Volunteering there meant helping with classes, sometimes setting up equipment, sometimes getting in the pool to demonstrate strokes, and sometimes just being an extra set of eyes to watch the kids while the instructor focused on one student. Whatever was needed, we did it. To this day, I can still smell the chlorine in that indoor pool and hear the water aerobics class.

> The lesson was always the same: if you find value in something, you give back.

That spirit of service followed me into high school, where I volunteered at the local science center, teaching birthday party science projects, and giving tours of the museum and butterfly garden. And it carried through into my college years at Virginia Tech.

At Virginia Tech, I became deeply involved in student activities, particularly with on-campus housing. At that time, about 9,100 students lived on campus, and I helped lead the governance and programming arm for all of them. The goal was simple: Make living on campus a positive experience. That wasn't always easy, since first-year students were required to live there, and many of them didn't want to. My volunteer role in this student organization meant working with Student Affairs professionals, student resident advisors, community directors, themed housing, and student leaders to plan retreats, conferences, service projects, and fun events.

One of my favorite projects was "Hokie Halloween," where we opened the residence halls to children from the community. Each living learning community and residence hall would transform into a haunted house (age-appropriate, of course), with face painting, pumpkin decorating, and games. It was about service, but also about bringing the Blacksburg and Virginia Tech communities together.

And then, everything changed on April 16, 2007, with the shooting I mentioned.

It started that morning in one of the residence halls and later moved into an academic building. Thirty-two classmates and professors were killed. For me, it shook everything. I had spent three years working to make campus a safe, positive place where students wanted to live, and suddenly that safety was shattered. The police sirens that echoed in my mind for months after, the pain of walking past those buildings. It is something I'll never forget.

In that moment, I leaned on the school's motto: *Ut Prosim*, or "That I May Serve." I had already lived by that motto, but after April 16th, it became my life's focus. Service wasn't just something I did anymore—it became who I was and wanted to be. I knew I had to live in a way that honored those thirty-two lives cut short.

That commitment to service has guided every decision I've made since then. It shows up in my involvement with bar associations, my volunteer work providing pro bono services, and my work with organizations like Legal Aid of North Carolina. It shows up to lead the Greensboro Bar Association, and I answer questions through the North Carolina Bar Foundation's Free Legal Answers program.

These are all different ways I've found to live out that passion, ways to serve my community using the strengths and skills I've developed as a family law attorney in North Carolina.

Giving Back

As I moved through my career, I kept thinking, *I can serve my community in so many ways*. And I'm part of a lot of different communities. I'm a woman. I'm a North Carolinian. I'm a lawyer. I'm a South Asian lawyer. I'm a South Asian *female* lawyer. So, what can I do to serve?

Early on, even back in law school, I felt a calling to help other women. Part of it came from not seeing many people who looked like me. I felt like an outlier. And then, when I finally became a licensed attorney, after struggling through the bar exam without much support from my alma mater, I knew I wanted to make things easier for the people coming behind me. I didn't want them to go through the same tunnel of muddied waters that I had to clear for myself.

So, I turned that passion toward serving women lawyers in North Carolina. It started with revitalizing our local women attorneys' group in Greensboro, in the Piedmont Triad. From there, I became involved statewide and ended up leading the North Carolina Association of Women Attorneys for two years. My message to women attorneys was simple: It doesn't matter how many times you took the bar exam or what your rank was in law school. What matters is what you *do* with the skills you have.

And I especially wanted South Asian women in North Carolina law schools to know they weren't just "the only one" or "the token." There is so much more to this profession and this community than that.

That focus on promoting women in the profession eventually connected me to the North Carolina Bar Association, the state's largest voluntary bar association, where I served as chair of the Women in the Profession Committee. And in that role, I helped to create the very first award in the bar association's history, specifically for women attorneys. Imagine that: a 14,000-member association, well over a hundred years old, and it took until 2024 to finally have an award recognizing women. For me, that was a big milestone, and it's one of the ways I try to show women law students, especially South Asian women, that yes, you can be seen and lead here.

In 2021, I was elected as a North Carolina State Bar Councilor for my judicial district in North Carolina. Now, a little context: North Carolina has 100 counties and forty-three judicial districts. Some of the smaller counties are grouped together, but Guilford County, where Greensboro is, has enough lawyers that we're split into two districts. The twenty-fourth Judicial District covers Greensboro and the northern part of the county.

Each judicial district has at least one elected councilor, elected by the licensed attorneys living in that district. I was elected at the end of 2021 to serve my first three-year term beginning in January 2022. The State Bar Council is the governing body of the North Carolina State Bar, which is our regulatory agency. There are sixty-six councilors (sixty-three attorney members and three non-lawyer public members appointed by the governor and other public officials) across the state. They're the ones who propose changes to the rules of professional conduct, issue ethics opinions, and discipline lawyers when necessary.

When I was elected, our judicial district had two Councilors. At that time, there were fewer than ten women on the council. I was also the youngest Councilor elected, and the only South Asian member, and still am. That matters because this is the body making decisions about our profession. It's important to have diverse voices and experiences at that table.

For example, family law looks very different from criminal defense or corporate law, and having someone who can say, "This is normal in family law," or "No, we don't do that," is important. Our perspectives shape the rules that guide the profession, and I want law students and young lawyers to see that people like them *can* be in those places where decisions are made, and their voices matter.

Part of my role is also bringing information back to my district, making sure people know what's going on with the NC State Bar. A lot of lawyers see the Bar as something scary or negative, like, "I don't want to hear from them, I must be in trouble." I want to change that perception. At the end of the day, yes, it's a state regulatory agency, but it's also just other lawyers who want the best for the profession.

That's what giving back looks like for me now: using my seat at the table to open the doors wider for others.

Serving people requires a deep commitment to walk alongside them during some of the most difficult moments of their lives. As you can see, those values are not formed in a courtroom. They are shaped through experience, perseverance, and the foundation of family and personal growth.

For many families, there is still work to be done after the last legal documents have been signed. Our focus now turns to what comes next—how people rebuild, move forward, and create a path toward stability, hope, and a new chapter of life after divorce.

CHAPTER 10

Planning for the Future

"Can I have sex with anybody now?"

A client recently asked me that question as we were discussing her divorce. She couldn't even look me in the eye.

Shortly after that, another client asked me if they were allowed to date now. In both cases, the answer was a resounding "Yes!"

I end up counseling clients on how to move forward, not only legally but also in life. So many of those personal decisions, like dating or relationships, can end up affecting the legal side of things, too.

Part of what I do is help people set up a plan for the future. Sometimes that's a financial plan, and sometimes it's more like a mental health plan. Because here's the thing: when we get licensed, our license literally says, "Attorney and Counsellor at Law." People often forget that second part, the "counsellor at law" part. But in family law, it comes up constantly. It's not just about the law. That counsellor role is a big part of how I serve my clients.

Now, I'm not a trained mental health professional, and I would never claim to be. But I am certified in mental health first aid by the National Council for Mental Wellness. I don't know if people realize that's even a thing, but it means I've been trained to recognize risks, know when to step in, and point people to the right resources. I chose to get that certification because of the volatile nature of family law and, honestly, for my own sake too.

For instance, one day I had a client meeting that ran late. At 12:45 p.m., my paralegal came into the conference room to remind me of a 1:00 p.m. appointment, and by 12:50, my phone buzzed with a reminder: "Therapist, 1 p.m." My client probably saw it, and for a second, I thought about hiding my phone. But then I thought, *No, I want them to see that I'm taking care of my own mental health too. That's important.*

One reason why I'm so aware of this is that a former client passed away by suicide after their family law matter was completed. Ever since then, I've been hyper-aware not only for my clients but also for myself and my staff. If a client suddenly stops responding to calls or emails, my first thought (this sounds awful, but it's true) isn't just that they're busy. We'll even try calling *67 or checking obituaries. It's morbid, but that's where my brain goes now. The hope, of course, is that it never comes to that.

So, when I say I serve my clients, I don't just mean pushing papers or showing up in court to argue. It's about protecting their legal interests, yes, but also helping them move into the next season of their life. (I don't really like saying "next chapter." I say "season.") Because the practice of law, at least in my world, is about serving people. Making sure their needs are actually met, not just legally, but as whole human beings.

Finding Hope

When I have a client who feels so hopeless about their legal issues that they just can't see a resolution or imagine things ever getting better, that's when the "counsellor at law" part of my job really comes into play.

I mentioned earlier that in North Carolina, our law licenses say "Attorney and Counsellor at Law," and I take that seriously. Because sometimes my role isn't just about the law; it's about shifting gears and asking, *What's actually going to be best for this client right now?*

Often, that means listening. Sometimes it's giving reassurance. Letting them know, even if they can't see it yet, that there will be an end to all of this conflict. I can't tell them exactly when, or exactly how it's going to unfold. But I can promise them that there *will* be a resolution.

Maybe it will be through collaborative law. Maybe through private mediation. Sometimes it's court-ordered mediation, or it could even be arbitration. And if none of those work, the last stop is a bench trial, a trial before a judge. One way or another, there will be closure.

The real questions are: "When do we get there?" "How do we get there?" and "What does it look like when we finally are there?"

How to Move Forward

As I mentioned, an important part of serving clients, for me, is helping them figure out how to move forward. That means setting up a plan for the future, sometimes a financial plan, sometimes a mental health plan. As a counsellor at law who's also trained to recognize mental health risks, I see this as an essential part of my role.

When I think about the long-term outlook for clients, it's especially important in collaborative or cooperative settings, whether we're talking mediation, non-litigation, or any of the many options people have for resolving family disputes. To me, anything that's an alternative to litigation, anything that moves away from that adversarial mindset, really benefits people in the long term. It gives spouses and co-parents the chance to look forward, to think beyond just what's happening right now.

That's a big part of my philosophy, my M.O. if you will. It's about helping people see beyond the immediate crisis, and when they can't, I hold that vision for them until they can. Often, by the time we reach the conclusion (everything signed, sealed, notarized, and stamped), clients can suddenly see further down the road than they ever thought possible six or twelve months earlier.

There's one case that always stands out in my mind. From the very beginning, both parents were laser-focused on their child. The very first agreement we reached was a parenting plan, basically their ground rules for co-parenting. And to everyone's surprise, it was the easiest part. They were eager to talk about it. The question wasn't "if" but "how." How would this work when they were living in two different towns and two different homes, with travel time between? They wanted to make sure their child's life stayed as stable as possible.

Once we had that parenting plan in place, it opened the door to everything else. We could then talk about finances: how the child's expenses would be covered, how daycare and after-school care would be paid for, and how their assets would be divided. They were a younger couple, so aside from a mortgage and student loans, they didn't have much debt. What they needed was a new financial structure and a new family plan that matched their new reality. And because we had already worked out co-parenting first, those financial discussions went much more smoothly.

By the end, they weren't just surviving the process. They were building something new. They moved into the same neighborhood, making it easy for their child to transition between homes. They each continued with work and finished graduate school, while also thriving as co-parents. They communicate civilly, they make decisions together, and while they're no longer in a romantic relationship, they share the most important role they'll ever have as co-parents.

That kind of outcome wasn't something I saw often when I was practicing traditional family law. But since moving into collaborative practice, it has become the norm for my clients. And honestly, to witness that transformation—it's one of the most refreshing parts of my work.

Divorce can be one of the most traumatic experiences that people go through in their lives, and while litigation is not always avoidable, a collaborative approach can take much of the trauma out of this difficult period and put some of the control back into your hands. It can seem like there is no light at the end of the tunnel, but there is always a way forward.

Choosing the Path Forward

If there's one thing I hope you take away from this book, it's this: family law is not just about the law. It's about real people navigating one of the most difficult transitions of their lives while trying to protect what matters most.

From the moment someone considers separation, every decision that follows has weight. Not just legal weight, but emotional, financial, and relational weight. The process you choose shapes the experience you live through. It affects how much control you keep, how much you spend, how long it takes, and how much damage—or healing—occurs along the way.

Throughout these chapters, I've walked you through the full landscape: collaborative family law, mediation, negotiation, alternative dispute resolution, the realities of dependents, and, when all else fails, litigation. None of these paths is inherently "right" or "wrong." Each exists for a reason. Sometimes, court intervention is necessary for safety or accountability. Other times, it's avoidable—and the cost of avoiding it can be measured not just in dollars saved, but in relationships preserved.

> What I've seen, again and again, is that families do best when they are given the tools, the space, and the permission to make their own decisions. When parents are able to step back from positional thinking and focus on the needs of their children, the outcomes are almost always better. Not perfect. Not painless. But better.

While this book is not meant to tell you what choice to make, my role, ethically and professionally, has always been to explain the options, lay out the risks and benefits, and help people make informed decisions. The same is true here. Knowledge is power in family law. Understanding the system allows you to navigate it with intention rather than fear.

If you are reading this while standing at the edge of separation, I want you to know this: you are not alone, and you are not powerless. Even in litigation, even in conflict, there are moments where choices can be made, offers can be extended, and paths can change. You are not required to surrender control simply because things feel overwhelming right now.

Family restructuring is never easy. But it doesn't have to be destructive. With the right process, the right professionals, and a willingness to focus on the future rather than relitigate the past, it is possible to move forward with dignity, clarity, and compassion.

At the end of the day, the law provides the framework—but *you* choose how your story unfolds.

Hopefully, you will choose to end your marriage peacefully.

References and Resources

- Manley, Elizabeth P., et al., eds. *Alternative Dispute Resolution in North Carolina: A New Civil Procedure*. 2nd ed. 2012.
- North Carolina Department of Health and Human Services. "Home Page." https://www.ncdhhs.gov.
- North Carolina Department of Health and Human Services. *N.C. Child Support Guidelines*. January 1, 2023. https://ncchildsupport.ncdhhs.gov/ecoa/cseGuideLines.htm.
- North Carolina General Statutes § 1-53 (2024).
- North Carolina General Statutes § 50 (2024).
- North Carolina General Statutes § 50A (2024).
- North Carolina General Statutes § 50B (2024).
- North Carolina General Statutes § 52C (2024).
- Rosenberg, Marshall B. *Nonviolent Communication: A Language of Life*. Edited by Lucy Leu. 3rd ed. 2015.

- Tesler, Pauline H. *Collaborative Law: Achieving Effective Resolution in Divorce Without Litigation.* 2nd ed. 2001.
- Webb, Stuart G., and Ronald D. Ousky. *The Collaborative Way to Divorce: The Revolutionary Method that Results in Less Stress, Lower Costs, and Happier Kids Without Going to Court.* 1st printing. 2007.

Glossary

50B, aka Domestic Violence Protective Order – Chapter 50B of the North Carolina General Statutes governs matters of domestic violence, and protective orders are often colloquially called "50Bs," whether they are temporary or permanent.

Alternative Dispute Resolution – A range of processes designed to assist parties in resolving conflicts outside of the traditional courtroom setting.

- **Negotiation** – The process of direct communication between the parties, either through their attorneys or personally, to reach an agreement. Negotiation can take place throughout the legal process, from initial discussions to settlement conferences, and can be facilitated by ADR professionals.
- **Mediation** – Mediation involves a neutral third party, known as a mediator, who facilitates discussions between the parties to help them reach a mutually acceptable agreement. The mediator does not make decisions but instead guides the conversation, promotes understanding, and assists in finding common ground.

    - Court-Ordered – When there is already a lawsuit filed and a Judge orders child custody mediation before a trial can occur, or is required in family financial cases (lawsuits with pending claims of equitable distribution and often alimony).
    - Private – When two parties in a domestic dispute/disagreement choose to work with a neutral third-party mediator to assist in resolving their disagreements. This often occurs before a lawsuit is filed or before the court issues any order requiring mediation and specific deadlines.
- **Arbitration** – A more formal ADR method, where a neutral third party, known as an arbitrator, is appointed to hear the case and make a binding decision. Arbitration can resemble a simplified version of a courtroom trial, with rules of evidence and a formal decision-making process.
- **Collaborative Family Law** – A voluntary and cooperative approach to dispute resolution. Each party has its own collaborative attorney, and all participants commit to resolving the issues without going to court. The process involves face-to-face meetings, where the parties and their attorneys work together to find creative solutions that meet the interests of all involved.

Cash Flow Worksheet – This tool is used to assess the needs of each person and the children by creating and reviewing individual budgets against the family's collective income for support purposes.

Child Custody – In North Carolina, the primary focus of child custody decisions is the best interests of the child. When determining child custody arrangements, the court considers several factors to ensure the child's well-being and promote a stable and nurturing environment.

- **Legal child custody** refers to a parent's right and responsibility to make important decisions regarding the child's upbringing, such as education, healthcare, religious affiliation, and extracurricular activities. Legal custody can be joint (shared by both parents) or sole (granted to one parent).
- **Physical child custody** relates to where the child will live and spend their time. It involves determining the primary residence of the child and the visitation or parenting time schedule for the noncustodial parent. Physical custody can be joint (shared physical custody) or sole (primary physical custody with visitation rights for the noncustodial parent).

Child Support – North Carolina has an income shares model of calculating child support, which is based on a number of different adjustments after looking at each parent's gross monthly income. Child support and child custody are two independent issues, and the only time custody affects child support is when choosing the appropriate worksheet or formula for calculating child support.

- North Carolina has child support guidelines, which are reviewed every four years, to assist in calculating child support. These guidelines consider the income of both parents, the number of children, and certain allowable expenses related to child-rearing.

Civil Collaborative Law training (fourteen hours) – While there is no statutory requirement for the number of hours for training as a civil collaborative attorney, the generally accepted practice is that collaboratively trained attorneys complete at least fourteen hours of basic and hands-on training. Different organizations in N.C provide basic and advanced training every year.

Collaborative Caucuses – These are breaks during collaborative Four-Way sessions where participants and their attorneys can break out one-on-one for discussion.

Collaborative Law Proceedings – The proceedings in family law matters (N.C.G.S. §50, Article 4). This is the specific statutory authority for collaborative law matters in family law cases.

Collaborative Neutrals – These are third parties that the collaborative participants jointly retain to assist them in working towards a resolution. Common examples of such neutrals are: Real Property Appraisers, Mediators, Financial Specialists, and Child Welfare Specialists.

Collaborative Participants – These are the spouses/co-parents and their respective attorneys who all sign a Collaborative Participation Agreement/Pledge.

Collaborative Pledge – This is the actual agreement, a binding contract, that all parties and their collaborative attorneys sign to begin the collaborative process. This Agreement will include language about full disclosure and how to end the collaborative process, among other things.

Department of Health and Human Services (DHHS) – The state agency that oversees many local departments and agencies that are applicable for family law matters in North Carolina (e.g., Department of Social Services and Vital Statistics).

Department of Social Services (DSS) – This is a local department that oversees public benefits, child protective services, adult protective services, child support enforcement, to name just a few.

Divorce (Simple, No-Fault, Absolute) – North Carolina is a "no-fault" divorce state, which means that couples can seek an absolute divorce without having to prove fault or wrongdoing on the part of either spouse.

Divorce from Bed and Board – This is essentially a court-ordered legal separation, used rarely when one party refuses to physically live separately and apart, and is only available under certain circumstances, like adultery and cruel and inhumane treatment, for example.

eCourts (Portal, File & Serve, Guide & File) – This is the North Carolina online portal for lawsuits filed in state courts, the mechanism for online filing of court papers, and Guide & File is a self-help option that the N.C Administrative Office of the Courts provides for North Carolinians with certain civil legal matters.

Equitable Distribution (ED) – The legal claim for division of marital and divisible assets and liabilities. There are a number of factors a court will consider when determining a fair division of the marital estate, with the underlying rebuttable presumption that equal is fair, meaning an equal 50-50 division starting point. Part of the division process is understanding the difference between marital property and separate property.

- **Marital Property** – Assets and debts acquired during the marriage.
- **Separate Property** – Assets and debts that belong solely to one spouse.

Four-Way Settlement Conference (also called collaborative sessions) – These are team meetings among the participants in a collaborative family law case. They are usually held every couple of weeks or as needed to work through the collaborative process together.

Friendly Lawsuit – When two people agree on how to resolve their legal issues but want a judge-signed court order, or one is required for some other purpose, one person can file a 'friendly' lawsuit as simply a mechanism to obtain the Court order.

Global Settlement – This is when two people (and their attorneys, if involved) choose to resolve all marital disputes together rather than piecemeal. Often, the compromises each person makes are dependent on the compromises of the other person.

Heartbalm Torts – These are civil actions between a spouse and a third party, not their separated/divorced spouse, that seek damages for the destruction of a marital relationship.

- **Alienation of Affection** – This is a lawsuit by one spouse against a third party for money damages arising from actions that alienated their spouse from a loving marriage. Often, this may be a paramour, family member, or possibly an employer.
- **Criminal Conversation** – This is a lawsuit by one spouse against a third party for money damages for sexual intercourse with their spouse while the spouses are married, prior to a legal separation.

Interest-Based Negotiation Model – This is the root of how the collaborative process differs from an adversarial/position-based negotiation model through litigation. Here, instead of focusing solely on results and achieving them at all costs, an interest-based model focuses on each person's interests and needs and how they can work to meet everyone's needs and interests.

Inventory Worksheet – This is for the division of **property**. It is a tool used to identify and evaluate the marital assets and liabilities, and problem-solving during collaborative meetings.

Legal Separation (also known as "separate maintenance") – Legal separation is when the latter of two things occur: one or both spouses no longer have the intent to live as a married couple, and the spouses live separately.

Litigation – This is the formal term for filing a lawsuit with a court to resolve a legal dispute.

Marital Misconduct – When a particular act occurs by one or both of the spouses after the date of marriage but prior to the date of separation, and is a factor when considering spousal support. A few examples are:

- **Illicit Sexual Behavior** – any sexual act with someone other than a person's spouse.
- **Abandonment** (Actual & Constructive) – Actual abandonment is when one spouse "leaves" the other physically without any reason or justification or prior communication. Constructive abandonment is when there is the withdrawal of love and affection from one spouse to the other.

NC Dispute Resolution Commission – "The North Carolina Dispute Resolution Commission was established in October of 1995, pursuant to N.C. Gen. Stat. § 7A-38.2. The Commission is charged primarily with certifying and regulating private mediators who serve the courts of this State. The Commission also recommends policy, rules, and rule revisions relating to dispute resolution in North Carolina's courts; provides support to court-based mediation programs; certifies mediation training programs; serves as a clearinghouse for information about court-based mediation programs; assists other State agencies interested in or providing dispute resolution services to their constituencies; publishes a newsletter and maintains this website."

Nonviolent Communication (NVC) – This is a method of communication that uses specific formulaic ways to communicate to reframe how to express one's individual needs while respecting the other person's needs. This method reframes and replaces defensive or attacking language during heavy, emotion-filled conversations.

Pleadings – This is the collective term for court-filed documents, which are public record; common examples are Complaint, Summons, an Answer & Counterclaims, and Divorce Judgement.

- **Stay of Litigation** – This is a formal hold on a court lawsuit to pursue alternative forms of dispute resolution.
- **Qualified Domestic Relations Order** – How we divide qualified retirement accounts prior to reaching retirement age without penalties.
- **Discovery** – The formal requests under the Rules of Civil Procedure to gather information and documents prior to a trial or hearing before a Judge.
- **Subpoena** – This is a request to a non-party for information, documents, and/or sworn testimony prior to a trial or hearing before a Judge.

Separation Agreement & Property Settlement – This is a private legal contract that resolves the marital legal issues related to a legal separation, such as property division, spousal support, children's issues (custody and support), and how to resolve future disagreements and/or disputes.

Spousal Support

- **Post-Separation Support** – Temporary financial support provided to a dependent spouse during the separation period but before a final resolution of the divorce. It is intended to address immediate financial needs and maintain the standard of living established during the marriage.

- **Alimony** – Ongoing financial support provided to a dependent spouse after the divorce is finalized. It is designed to assist the spouse in maintaining a similar lifestyle enjoyed during the marriage and to help them become financially self-sufficient.
  - Permanent alimony
  - Rehabilitative alimony

Uniform Child Custody Jurisdiction Enforcement Act (N.C.G.S. §50A) – UCCJEA is the act adopted throughout the USA by each state about which state has jurisdiction over child custody cases and how states can enforce or modify child custody court orders issued by a different state.

Uniform Civil Collaborative Law Act (N.C.G.S. §1, Article 53) – This is the statutory framework on civil collaborative matters as a method of alternative dispute resolution.

Uniform Interstate Family Support Act (N.C.G.S. §52C) – UIFSA is the act adopted throughout the USA by each state regarding the enforcement and modification of family support court orders by a state that did not issue the original order.

Author's Note

Divorce is often described as the end of something. In truth, it is also a beginning.

When I began practicing family law in North Carolina, I quickly saw that while divorce is a legal process, it is profoundly human at its core. Behind every file or case number is a family navigating uncertainty, grief, fear, and hope, often all at once. Too many people believe that divorce must be adversarial, destructive, and financially or emotionally devastating. That belief, unfortunately, becomes reality when couples are not shown another way.

Collaborative divorce offers that other way.

This book was written for individuals who want to move through divorce with dignity, clarity, and intention, especially when children are involved. It is also for spouses who value privacy, respect, and long-term stability over courtroom conflict. My goal is not simply to explain the collaborative process in North Carolina, but to empower you with knowledge so you can make informed decisions about your future.

Peaceful does not mean painless. But it does mean purposeful.

If this guide helps even one family transition with less conflict, less fear, and more understanding, then it has done its job.

Manisha

Acknowledgments

No professional work—and certainly no book—is created alone.

Thank you, Melanie (and your team), for helping bring this vision to life. When I first shared what I hoped to create, you embraced it wholeheartedly and gave me the tools and guidance to shape it into this final work. I could not be prouder of what we have created or more hopeful about what this book will mean to those facing one of the most difficult seasons of their lives.

I am deeply grateful to the clients who have entrusted me with some of the most vulnerable moments of their lives. Your courage, resilience, and commitment to your families inspire me daily. While confidentiality prevents me from naming you, this book exists because of what I have learned from walking alongside you.

Thank you to Chief Justice Cheri Beasley for taking the time to read my manuscript and so graciously agreeing to contribute the Foreword. Your words ring true to the spirit of this book and your dedication to the North Carolina judicial system and legal profession is something I aspire to.

To the many leaders and mentors who have shaped me over the past two decades, thank you for instilling in me a commitment to service, professionalism, and thoughtful innovation, in both life and the practice of law. You modeled what it truly means to lead with purpose, integrity, and steadiness. You showed me that powerful leadership is rooted not in opposition, but in calm strength, resilience, and collaboration, the same foundation upon which this book is built. Yolanda, Janet Ward, and Ronda, your guidance has profoundly influenced the leader, lawyer, and businesswoman I have become. I am deeply grateful for your wisdom, your example, and your unwavering belief in me.

To my colleagues in the legal and collaborative family law community across North Carolina: thank you for your integrity and dedication to a better model of dispute resolution. The collaborative process works because of professionals who believe families deserve solutions, not battles. I am especially appreciative of the mental health professionals, financial neutrals, and fellow attorneys who make the collaborative process possible. Your expertise ensures that families receive comprehensive support, not just legal answers.

To my paralegal, Kayla Harris: thank you for your tireless work, your compassion for our clients, and your unwavering commitment to excellence. This book reflects the standard we strive to uphold every day.

Beyond the courtroom and the office, I have been sustained by friendships that have shaped who I am: Adrienne, Derrick, Carlie, and Christon. From college days to moving to a new state, through the long nights of law school, the leap of opening my own firm, and even through cancer, you four have been my constants. You have supported every dream, steadied every doubt, and stood beside me without judgment—only love, honesty, and unwavering encouragement. Your friendship has shown me that peace does not mean the absence of challenge, but the presence of strength, resilience, and grit, the very qualities that make new beginnings possible.

And finally, to my parents, Smita and Pravin Patel: thank you for your steady love and support over the past forty years, which made all of this possible. I would not be where I am without you. You may not always have understood every turn in my path, even those teenage years when all I could talk about was becoming a lawyer, but I hope you know that I am walking in the calling I have long felt on my heart. I am living the very lesson you taught me from the beginning: that our greatest purpose is to serve.

It is because of each of you that I believe endings, when handled with intention and courage, can become the beginning of something peaceful and whole.

With gratitude and love,

Manisha

About the Author

Manisha Patel is known for combining deep legal expertise with a calm, practical, and compassionate approach that helps clients make good decisions in some of the most stressful moments of their lives. As a collaborative family law attorney, certified mediator, and founder of a boutique family law firm in Greensboro, North Carolina, Manisha focuses on helping families navigate separation, divorce, and co-parenting with less conflict and more clarity, using collaborative law and mediation to keep people out of courtroom battles whenever possible. She is an elected Councilor to the North Carolina State Bar and past President of the Greensboro Bar Association, as well as a longtime leader in organizations that support women in the legal profession, pro bono service, and lawyer wellness.

Manisha's practice is devoted exclusively to family law. She works with clients facing divorce, custody and support issues, adoption, and family agreements, and she is especially drawn to cases where thoughtful communication and structured problem-solving can change the trajectory of a family's future. Her goal is not just to resolve legal issues, but to help people understand their options, lower the emotional temperature, and move forward with solutions they can live with long after the legal process ends.

Clients often describe Manisha as steady, clear, and deeply prepared. She believes that when people feel informed and supported, they make better decisions—for themselves and for their children. That belief shapes both her legal work and her commitment to alternatives to traditional litigation.

Manisha earned her law degree from Elon University School of Law and holds bachelor's degrees in Economics and History from Virginia Tech. She is licensed to practice in all North Carolina state courts and in the United States District Court for the Middle District of North Carolina.

In addition to her client work, Manisha has spent years in leadership roles within the legal community, contributing to the profession through bar service, advocacy for women lawyers, and community engagement.

Professional Leadership & Recognition:

- Elected Councilor, 24th Judicial District, North Carolina State Bar
- Past President, Greensboro Bar Association
- Past President, North Carolina Association of Women Attorneys
- Appointed Representative of the National Conference of Women's Bar Associations to the American Bar Association

Commission on Women in the Profession
- Member, North Carolina Bar Association
- Member, American Bar Association
- Board Member, National Conference of Women's Bar Associations
- Licensed to practice in all North Carolina State Courts
- Licensed to practice in the U.S. District Court for the Middle District of North Carolina
- Named Super Lawyers Rising Stars (multiple years)
- Recognized in Business North Carolina's Legal Elite for Family Law (multiple years)

In her free time, Manisha loves to travel, workout, and spend time with the light of her life, her pup Rusty M. Patel.

www.ingramcontent.com/pod-product-compliance
Lightning Source LLC
LaVergne TN
LVHW090401210926
848480LV00002B/413
9798993549309